Harvey The Musical

—∾—

Save the Kids!

Andrew J. McNabb

ISBN-13: 9781492839170
ISBN-10: 1492839175
Library of Congress control Number: 2013921177
CreateSpace Independent Publishing Platform
North Charleston, South Carolina

Preface

People like mysteries. How about one of the greatest mysteries of the 20th century? Here is the ultimate "cold case."

People like spy stories. How about intrigue with the CIA and the KGB at the height of the Cold War? Throw in some Cuban spies, trips to exotic places, the president of the United States in danger, and the threat of World War III.

People like colorful characters. There are FBI agents, the Mafia, the stunningly gorgeous KGB Gal, the enigmatic F, G, and A - and they are not even the main characters.

People like music. How about a musical with songs based on classic hits by legendary performers of the era? The Beatles, Rolling Stones, Animals, Monkees, Rare Earth, Johnny Rivers, Alice Cooper, and more - even Ozzie Osbourne contributes.

People like dancing. The choreographers can unleash their creativity with a variety of settings and moods that range from a light hearted 50's Sock Hop to a ghoulish performance reminiscent of Dante's Inferno. There is even a dance totally in the dark.

Put it all together and we have a very entertaining evening with a musical called "Harvey."

But wait, there is more to the story.

Our daughters enjoyed performing on their high school drill team - the Brazoswood Buccaneers. When they went away to college, they missed performing. Their high school friends also missed being in the spot light. They asked if I could write something for them for when they got together during college breaks.

Recognizing that our kids would soon leave the nest, I wanted to share with them worldly observations and give them a "heads up" on what they might face in the real world.

How does a parent do this? I saw three alternatives:

1. Sit down and give them advice. Would you have listened at that age?

2. Write a self-help book. Would they ever read the book?

    or,

3. Hide the messages I wanted to share in a parable.

So I subtly shared my advice and worldly observations in "Harvey The Musical - Save The Kids!" Hopefully they picked up on the advice and observations (if not, I may be writing a self-help book!) And yes, our daughters and their friends returned to the stage in multiple "Harvey" parties at our house.

I hope you enjoy the book, but above all, remember the cause - we have to SAVE THE KIDS!

Andrew J. McNabb
10/30/2013

Major Characters

HARVEY: Leading male character, born in Texas, initially 18 years old, always wears blue jeans and a white tee shirt, grew up in a dysfunctional home, high school drop out, ordinary looking, introspective, very adaptable to new situations. Is he the most famous secret agent of the 20th century?

MARINA: Leading female character, born in the Soviet Union, initially 17 years old, dresses conservatively - can't afford nice clothes, has lived with her uncle's family the last several years after her mother's tragedy, nice looking, smart, witty, energetic, pragmatic. At the age of 22, can she stop World War III?

CIA 1: Approximately 40 years old, leader of the CIA field station, always wears black pants and a short sleeve blue turtle neck shirt

CIA 2: Approximately 30 years old, second in command of the CIA field station, always wears black pants and a short sleeve blue turtle neck shirt

KGB 1: Approximately 40 years old, leader of the KGB field station, always wears black pants and a short sleeve red turtle neck shirt

KGB 2: Approximately 30 years old, second in command of the KGB field station, always wears black pants and a short sleeve red turtle neck shirt

CUBA 1: Approximately 40 years old, leader of the Cuban spy station, always wears a straw hat, tropical shirt, shorts, and has a cigar in his hand, speaks with a fake Spanish accent

CUBA 2: Approximately 30 years old, second in command of the Cuban spy station, always wears a straw hat, tropical shirt, shorts, and has a cigar in his hand, speaks with a fake Spanish accent

MAFIA 1: Approximately 40 years old, leader of the local Mafia group, always wears black pants, a long sleeve black pullover shirt, and a black hat, speaks with a fake Italian accent

MAFIA 2: Approximately 30 years old, second in command of the local Mafia group, always wears black pants, a long sleeve black pullover shirt, and a black hat, speaks with a fake Italian accent

FBI 1: Approximately 40 years old, leader of the FBI special project field station, always wears a blue suit with a white shirt and narrow black tie, very nerdy

FBI 2: Approximately 30 years old, second in command of the FBI special project field station, always wears a blue suit with a white shirt and narrow black tie, very nerdy

F: A personification, appears to be approximately 20 years old, quirky, always wears blue jeans and a white tee shirt with a large red letter "F" on the front and back

G: A personification, appears to be approximately 20 years old, quirky, always wears blue jeans and a white tee shirt with a large red letter "G" on the front and back

A: A personification, appears to be approximately 20 years old, quirky, always wears blue jeans and a white tee shirt with a large red letter "A" on the front and back

KGB GAL: Approximately 25 years old, gorgeous blonde, always wears suggestive outfits, men find her irresistible, speaks with a fake Russian accent

KGB COLONEL: Approximately 50 years old, leader of a large KGB group in Minsk, Soviet Union, wears a military uniform, a big grizzly man, very tough but has a soft spot for his niece Marina that came to live with his family

JACK: Approximately 50 years old, Dallas night club operator, chubby, wears a brown suit with a brown hat that has a black band, a loner

DETECTIVE: Approximately 35 years old, good looking, very ambitious, a smooth talker, wears a white suit with a blue shirt and red tie

List of Songs

Act 1

1. "Can't You See What's Going On?" based on "For What It's Worth" written and performed by Buffalo Springfield

2. "For The Kids" based on "For Your Love" written by Graham Gouldman and performed by The Yardbirds

3. "I'm Only Eighteen" based on "I'm Eighteen" written and performed by Alice Cooper

4. "Secret Agent" based on "Secret Agent Man" written by Steve Barri and P.F. Sloan and performed by Johnny Rivers

5. "Rock Around The Clock" written by Max C. Freedman and James E. Myers

6. "Tell Me About Your New Plane" based on "Hello I Love You" written by Jim Morrison and performed by The Doors

7. "Going to the USSR" based on "Back to the USSR" written by Paul McCartney and performed by The Beatles

8. "Here Come The Commies" based on "Theme From The Monkees" written by Tommy Boyce and Bobby Hart and performed by the Monkees

9. "My Russian Girl" based on "Sugar, Sugar" written by Andy Kim and Jeff Barry and performed by The Archies

10. "We're Going to Texas" based on "Deep In The Heart Of Texas" written by June Hershey and Don Swander

11. "House Where Evil Deeds Are Done" based on the folk song "House Of The Rising Sun" as performed by The Animals

12. "The Spinning Wheel Guy" based on "Spinning Wheel" written by David Clayton-Thomas and performed by Blood, Sweat, and Tears

13. "For The Kids" based on "For Your Love" written by Graham Gouldman and performed by The Yardbirds

14. "It's Not For The Kids" based on "Can't Buy Me Love" written by Paul McCartney and performed by The Beatles

Act 2

1. "Hidden Hands" based on "Rock On" written and performed by David Essex

2. "Lonely World" based on "Eleanor Rigby" written by Paul McCartney and John Lennon and performed by The Beatles

3. "I'm No Longer A Teen" based on "I'm Eighteen" written and performed by Alice Cooper

4. "FGA Lite" based on the American folk song "Shortening Bread"

5. "FGA Heavy" based on "Fire" written by Ozzie Osborne and performed by Black Sabbath

6. "When Black Friday Comes" based on "Black Friday" written and performed by Steely Dan

7. "Are You Going to Assassinate?" based on "Are You Going to Celebrate?" written and performed by Rare Earth

8. "My Intentions Are Good" based on "Don't Let Me Be Misunderstood" written by Benjamin/Marcus/Caldwell and performed by The Animals

9. "Where Did I Go Wrong?" based on "How Can I Be Sure?" written and performed by The Rascals

10. "Harvey" based on "Angie" written and performed by The Rolling Stones

11. "It's Not For The Kids" based on "Can't Buy Me Love" written by Paul McCartney and performed by The Beatles

12. "Save The Kids!" based on "Louie, Louie" written and performed by The Kingsmen

Curtain Call

"Secret Agent" based on "Secret Agent Man" written by Steve Barri and P.F. Sloan and performed by Johnny Rivers

For Jennifer, Kristin, and friends

ACT 1

Scene One

A large video screen is in the center of the stage. The house lights dim. Black and white pictures of children from the 1950's are shown on the screen. Sounds of happy children laughing and playing are heard. Pictures and video clips of children TV shows from the 1950's follow - The Lone Ranger, Captain Kangaroo, Howdy Doody, Lamb Chops, Leave it to Beaver. The Lone Ranger is shown several times. Next are pictures of kids with toy guns playing Cowboys vs. Indians and war games.

This is followed by video clips from the era of soldiers marching, military jets being launched from aircraft carriers, and the firing of various guns and artillery. Franklin Delano Roosevelt is heard saying, "The only thing we have to fear is fear itself."

Pictures from the 1950's are shown - cars, fashions, baseball stars, musicians, Dwight Eisenhower, John F. Kennedy, Nikita Khrushchev, Fidel Castro, and Marilyn Monroe. John F. Kennedy is heard saying, "Ask not what your country can do for you, but what you can do for your country."

Newspaper headlines are shown - Sputnik launched, the U2 spy plane, the Bay of Pigs, the Cuban missile crisis, Lee Harvey Oswald holding a gun, the JFK motorcade in Dallas, JFK shot, Oswald shot, LBJ being sworn in as the new president.

The video screen is raised and the spotlight shines on a lone Troubadour on the front right of the stage, between the closed curtain and the front edge of the stage. The Troubadour is colorfully dressed as a court jester. A crowd of people with protest signs are on the left side of the stage. Four men carrying rifles and dressed in blue jeans and white tee shirts appear in the audience. They walk up to the stage and go behind the curtain during the song.

The music starts for "Can't You See What's Going On?" based on "For What It's Worth" written and performed by Buffalo Springfield.

TROUBADOUR

There's something happening here
What it is ain't exactly clear

(raises one finger and points to four men with guns
walking towards the stage)

There's a man with a gun over there
Telling me I got to beware

CAST

I think it's time we stop, children, what's that sound?
Everybody look - what's going down?

TROUBADOUR

There's battle lines being drawn
Nobody's right if everybody's wrong

Young people speaking their minds
Getting so much resistance from behind

CAST

It's time we stop, hey, what's that sound?
Everybody look - what's going down?

TROUBADOUR

What a field-day for the heat
A thousand people in the street

(crowd raises and lowers signs)

Singing songs and carrying signs
Mostly say, "hooray for our side"

CAST

It's time we stop, hey, what's that sound?
Everybody look - what's going down?

TROUBADOUR

Paranoia strikes deep
Into your life it will creep
It starts when you're always afraid
You step out of line, the man come and take you away

(Police 1 and Police 2 come on stage and remove
two of the protesters)

CAST

We better stop, hey, what's that sound?
Everybody look - what's going down?

Stop, hey, what's that sound?
Everybody look - what's going down?

Stop, now, what's that sound?
Everybody look - what's going down?

Stop, children, what's that sound?
Everybody look - what's going down?

(spot light off, curtain opens)

Scene Two

Outside the US military base. The stage is split with two similar offices. On the left is the KGB office with a large Soviet flag, a desk, and two chairs. On the right is the CIA office with a large American flag, a desk, and two chairs. KGB 1 and KGB 2 are dressed in black pants and short sleeve red turtle neck shirts. CIA 1 and CIA 2 are dressed in black pants with short sleeve blue turtle neck shirts. The lights are initially off on both sides of the stage.

NARRATOR

Hidden hands behind the scenes
Come together to make others dreams
Creating fortunes, crowning kings
Hidden hands, never seen.

Come with me on a journey. For some it will be a new adventure. For others, it will be a chance to revisit events of their youth.

The year is 1958. The world is trembling with fear. The United States and Soviet Union each possess an arsenal of atomic weapons. The Soviet Union has launched Sputnik, a communications satellite that passes over the United States. The United States has developed the U2 spy plane that flies high above the antiaircraft guns of the Soviet Union.

Our first stop is Atsugi, Japan – the home base for the U2 spy plane. It is now the hot spot for the world's intelligence agencies. The Soviet KGB spy agency wants information on the U2 spy plane that can be used to shoot it down. The American CIA spy agency realizes this and is trying to keep the secrets from the Soviets.

(Lights brighten on KGB side of stage, but remain off on the CIA side. KGB 1 is sitting behind the desk. KGB 2 is sitting in a visitor chair.)

KGB 1

Welcome back comrade. How are things in Moscow?

KGB 2

Chilly, very chilly comrade. The American U2 spy plane is causing many problems.

KGB 1

So, tell me the latest.

KGB 2

With the spy planes, the Americans can learn too much. They can follow our military movements, they can tell how much are factories are producing...

KGB 1

Yes, yes. But we know the Americans have agents on the ground that can do this as well.

KGB 2

True, but the latest worries are what the spy plane can do to the morale of our civilians. What happens when the Americans start taking pictures of our towns, our streets, our houses? We will lose our privacy. Can you imagine what it would be like for people on the other side of the world to be able to see your house, to see the street where you live? And where does it stop? Our people will feel like they are always being watched.

KGB 1

 They are always being watched. We're the KGB and we are doing the watching.

KGB 2

Yes, you know that and I know that, but our people are afraid...

KGB 1

And if we can't protect them, there will be protests, and riots - they will revolt and the country will fall apart.

KGB 2

Yes, it is important to either keep them happy or so busy that they have no time to think. So what is the plan to get information on the U2 spy plane?

KGB 1

The plan is simple comrade - we get the Americans at the U2 base to talk.

KGB 2

And how do we do that? Bribes? Torture? Oh I know some people that are great at torture, and they really enjoy doing it!

KGB 1

Much too gruesome and not always effective. What I propose is simple and always works - we give the young men what they want.

KGB 2

And that is?

KGB 1

What young men always want – wine and women. Get alcohol in a guy and put him in front of a cute girl and he will tell her everything.

(Lights dim on the KGB side of the stage and bright-
en on the CIA side. CIA 1 is sitting behind the desk.
CIA 2 is sitting in a visitor chair.)

CIA 1

Welcome back my friend. How are things in Washington?

CIA 2

Chilly, very chilly. Sputnik has everyone scared.

CIA 1

So tell me the latest.

CIA 2

People are worried that Sputnik might fall out of orbit and crash in the US or the Soviets might put an atomic bomb in space that could be dropped on our cities.

CIA 1

They have planes that could just as easily drop bombs or crash into our cities.

CIA 2

True, but the American people think their government can protect them from everything. If they lose faith in the government, they will be upset, things could get real ugly, and...

CIA 1

I know, I know. They may even elect a Democrat president.

CIA 2

Exactly. So what is the solution?

CIA 1

To Sputnik, it is easy - you build a rocket and fly to the moon.

CIA 2

(sarcastically)

Yeah, right. Maybe grab some cheese and see little green men in flying saucers along the way.

CIA 1

I know that is totally far-fetched, but somehow we have to show our people, and the rest of the world, that we are just as good or better at the rocket stuff.

CIA 2

Eventually we will do that. But in the meantime, we have to make the people at home feel good So how do we do that?

CIA 1

By showing them that they are better off than the Soviets.

CIA 2

(nodding)

Of course, if you can't make things better for your side, tell your people the other guys have it much worse, and they'll feel better.

CIA 1

Exactly. We tell them that Americans are much better off and that we are watching the Soviets with the U2, the most advanced spy plane ever created!

CIA 2

This area is crawling with Soviet spies. It is just a matter of time before they get information on the U2 spy plane that they can use to shoot it down. How are we going to stop them? There are too many people. Loose lips sink ships as the saying goes.

CIA 1

Stop them? The best way to stop them is to give them the information.

CIA 2

Say what!? Have you gone mad, man?

CIA 1

We give them false information - spread lies, or, as we like to call it, misinformation. We give them some good information and some bad information and it will take them years to separate the good from the bad.

CIA 2

So how do we do it?

CIA 1

We need to find a dupe. Someone very gullible, not too smart, that will work with us. We give him the information and he passes it to the Soviets.

(Lights dim on the CIA side of the stage and
brighten on the KGB side)

KGB 2

Wine and women comrade - yes, the plan is brilliant! If I may, I have a personal question for you. You have been doing this job for many years. Why do you do it? What motivates you to do what you do?

KGB 1

That comrade, is a question I think all men ask. I have asked myself that many times. Some might say for money or fame, maybe power, or patriotism. For civilians it might be loyalty to one's company.

KGB 2

But how about you?

KGB 1

Oh, I could say it is for my wife, who is thousands of miles away. No, I think I do what I do for the kids. I do it so they can grow up in a world that is safe and free from fear. Yes, it is for the kids!

> (KGB 1 and KGB 2 walk to the middle of the stage
> and pretend to be looking out a window facing the
> CIA side of the stage. They freeze in place as the
> lights brighten on the CIA side.)

CIA 2

A misinformation campaign my friend - yes, the plan is brilliant! If I may, I have a personal question for you. You have been doing this job for many years. Why do you do it? What motivates you to do what you do?

CIA 1

That my friend, is a question I think all men ask. I have asked myself that many times. Some might say for money or fame, maybe power, or patriotism. For civilians it might be loyalty to one's company.

CIA 2

But how about you?

Oh, I could say it is for my wife, who is thousands of miles away. No, I think I do what I do for the kids. I do it so they can grow up in a world that is safe and free from fear. Yes, it is for the kids!

(CIA1 and CIA2 walk to the middle of the stage and pretend to be looking out the window facing the KGB side of the stage. They are opposite their KGB counterparts and make motions with their hands, arms, and legs that are copied by their counterparts. The music starts and they sing "For the Kids" based on "For Your Love" written by Graham Gouldman and performed by The Yardbirds. During the "I'll kill anything in sight" parts of the song they pull out guns and aim at their counterparts.)

CIA 1, CIA 2, KGB 1, KGB 2

For the Kids

For the Kids

For the Kids
I'll give them everything and more, and that's for sure
For the Kids
I'll bring them Barbie dolls and go karts to their door
For the Kids
I will use all my might
And take on any fight

(guns out)

I'll kill anything in sight
So they can sleep safe at night

(next three "Kids" are drawn out)

For the Kids
For the Kids
For the Kids

For the Kids, for the Kids
I will give the stars above
For the Kids, for the Kids
I will give them all I can

For the Kids

For the Kids

For the Kids
I'd give the moon if it were mine to give
For the Kids
I'd give the stars and the sun 'fore I live
For the Kids
I will use all my might
And take on any fight

(guns out)

I'll kill anything in sight
So they can sleep safe at night

(next four "Kids" are drawn out)

For the Kids
For the Kids
For the Kids
For the Kids

(lights dim)

Scene Three

Later the same day in the barracks of the US military base. On the back left side of the stage is a large American flag, on the back right side of the stage is a window, there are five cots on the left side of the stage with a pillow on each cot. There are storage trunks on the ground at the end of each cot. The door to the barracks is on the right side. There are four GI's and Harvey. The GI's are getting ready to go out. Two are shirtless, one is looking in a mirror and combing his greasy hair, and one is sitting on a cot tying his shoes. During the scene the GI's finish getting dressed in their military uniforms. Harvey is dressed in blue jeans with a white tee shirt and is sitting on his cot reading a book.

GI 1

(draws out second syllable of "party")

We are going to party tonight!

GI 2

The studs are going to be in action!

GI 3

Studs? You mean THE stud - that's me, and have I got the moves.

(makes a cool move, draws out "Hey")

Hey!

GI 4

Moves? The only moves you are going to make is to be on your knees begging me for a piece of the action.

(gets on his knees, draws out "please")

Please, see if they have a friend for me. I'll take anything. A grandmother, a great grandmother…

GI 1

(jumps to his knees, draws out "Baa")

Or maybe a nice sheep or goat - Baa!

(GI 1, GI 2, GI 3, and GI 4 laugh, scuffle, and
then look over at Harvey)

GI 2

Hey Harvey, get ready to go. The dames are awaiting.

GI 3

Yeah and like why are you always reading?

HARVEY

I'm, I'm not sure guys. Do you ever have doubts?

GI 4

Doubts about dames? Are you trying to tell us that you are...

(motions his hands up and down in a wavy motion)

HARVEY

Oh that? Oh no. I like women as much as the next guy. No, I'm wondering why we are here. Why is our side better than their side?

GI 1

Hey man, we're Americans. We're always right.

HARVEY

But, what if we're wrong?

GI 2

Can't be - like the song says

God Bless America

God likes us man – cause we are right.

GI 3

Harvey, you think too much. All we need to do is what we are told. The generals, the President they make the decisions and we follow the orders.

GI 4

And when we're not following orders, bring on the dames and booze!

HARVEY

But what if they are leading us down a wrong path?

GI 1

(putting his arm around Harvey)

Harvey, Harvey think of it this way. Do you think fifty years from now history will remember any of us? Oh they may remember a president and maybe a general or two, but nobody is going to know what we thought or did.

GI 2

Wine, women, and song. That's the only way to go!

GI 3

Now that's what I call deep thinking. I'll vote for you for President any day.

(dressed and ready to leave, the GI's turn
back to look at Harvey)

GI 4

Harvey, are you going with us?

HARVEY

Maybe, maybe some other time.

(The GI's leave. Harvey paces for a moment. The lights dim and the spotlight is directed at Harvey as he sings "I'm Only Eighteen" based on "I'm Eighteen" by Alice Cooper. Near the end of the song, CIA 1 and CIA 2 are seen walking by the barracks window at the back right of the stage. They pass by the window, stop, and go back to the window and watch. At the end of the song, they go inside the barracks, shake Harvey's hand, and escort him off the right side of the stage.)

Lines form on my face and hands
Lines form from the ups and downs
I'm in the middle without any plans
I'm a boy and I'm a man

I'm eighteen
And I don't know what I want
Eighteen
I just don't know what I want
Eighteen
I gotta get away
I gotta get out of this place
I'll go runnin in outer space
Oh yeah

I got a
Baby's brain and an old man's heart
Took eighteen years to get this far
Don't always know what I'm talking about
Feels like I'm living in the middle of doubt
Cause I'm
Eighteen
I get confused every day
Eighteen
I just don't know what to say
Eighteen
I gotta get away

(CIA 1 and CIA 2 are seen at the window at the
back right of the stage)

Lines form in the East and the West
Lines form on the Left and Right
I'm in the middle
The middle of life
I'm a boy and I'm a man
I'm eighteen and I don't know

Oh I don't know

Cause I don't know
Can't know
Don't know
Can't know
Don't know
Help me
Eighteen
Eighteen and I don't know

(CIA 1 and CIA 2 walk inside the barracks,
shake Harvey's hand, and escort him off
stage as the lights dim.)

Scene Four

In the CIA office the same day. There is a large American flag on the wall. The office has one desk and two chairs. CIA 1 is sitting in one chair behind the desk and Harvey is sitting in the other chair. CIA 2 is standing.

CIA 1

Son, tell us about yourself.

HARVEY

Well, well sir my name is Harvey and I'm from Ft. Worth, Texas. I'm an Aviation Electronics Operator. My squad is assisting with the U2 plane.

CIA 2

How about family?

HARVEY

Sir, I have a mother, a brother, and a step brother. My father died two months before I was born.

CIA 1

It must have been rough growing up.

HARVEY

It was sir. Mother did her best, but we didn't have much money. There were times she had to put us in orphanages, but she always came back for us when she had more money. She remarried - an electrical engineer. Things were good for a while, until she caught him in bed with a broad.

CIA 2

How long you been in the service?

HARVEY

Almost two years, sir. I enlisted six days after my seventeenth birthday. I tried to enlist at sixteen, but they told me I had to wait until I turned seventeen. I knew I was under the age limit, but believe me sir, I just had to get away. There was no life for me in Ft. Worth and I really want to serve my country.

                (The CIA agents look at each other,
                        smile, and nod)

CIA 1

You have certain skills that are highly valued in our line of work.

HARVEY

Skills? Sir, I work hard and will serve my country well, but skills? I never even finished the tenth grade.

CIA 1

True, but you have what we like to call adaptation skills.

CIA 2

You have the ability to adjust to changing environments.

HARVEY

(looking puzzled)

Excuse me, sir?

CIA 1

Son, we have a very special top secret mission - just for you. It is a tough job. It is an opportunity to serve your country and your country really needs you.

CIA 2

(draws out "real")

It's a very manly job. You can show the world you are a real man!

CIA 1

You'll be a legend.

CIA 2

You'll be a secret agent!

(The music starts to "Secret Agent" based on "Secret Agent Man" written by Steve Barri and P.F. Sloan and performed by Johnny Rivers. The two CIA agents sing and dance a duet for the first part of the song while Harvey watches. KGB Gal joins them during "pretty faces" and dances amorously with CIA 1 and CIA 2. Harvey joins in the singing and dancing near the end of the song.)

CIA 1

There's a man who leads a life of danger

CIA 2

To everyone he meets he stays a stranger

CIA 1

With every move he makes another chance he takes

CIA 2

Odds are he won't live to see tomorrow

CIA 1 & CIA 2

Secret Agent Man
Secret Agent Man
They've given you a number and taken away your name

(KGB GAL enters and dances amorously with
CIA 1 and CIA 2)

CIA 1

Beware of pretty faces that you find

CIA 2

A pretty face can hide an evil mind

CIA 1

Oh be careful what you say

CIA 2

Or you will give yourself away

KGB GAL

Odds are you won't live to see tomorrow

(Harvey joins the dancing)

CIA 1, CIA 2, KGB GAL

Secret Agent Man
Secret Agent Man
They've given you a number and taken away your name

Secret Agent Man
Secret Agent Man
They've given you a number and taken away your name

CIA 1

Swinging nightlife in Clute, Texas one day

CIA 2

Spying undercover in Russia after that

CIA 1

Oh be careful what you say

CIA 2

Or you will give yourself away

KGB GAL

Odds are you won't live to see tomorrow

Secret Agent Man
Secret Agent Man
They've given you a number and taken away your name
Secret Agent Man

HARVEY

Wow! I'm going to be a real secret agent!

(lights dim)

Scene Five

In a Japanese night club that evening. In the back left corner of the stage is a bar and a bartender. KGB 1 and KGB 2 are sitting at a table in the back right corner of the stage. Four gals in 1950's "sock hop" outfits are sitting at a table on the front right corner of the stage. A colorful light is swirling on the left side of the stage. "Rock Around the Clock" is playing softly and there are two couples dancing in the back center of the stage. The four GI's are dressed in their military uniforms and enter the stage from the left. They stop, look around the club, point to the four gals, and then huddle to talk among themselves. The gals huddle after seeing the GI's. GI 3 and GAL 3 walk to the middle of the stage. GI 3 is nervous.

GI 3

(doing a very weak cool guy imitation,
softly draws out "Hey")

Hey.

GAL 3

I like your moves. Do you want to dance?

(They walk to the back center of the stage and start
to dance. The remaining GI's point at them and smile
and then sheepishly walk toward the three gals who
are walking towards them. They meet in the front
center of the stage.)

GI 1

(to GAL 1, doing an even weaker cool guy imitation,
slightly draws out "Hey")

Hey.

GAL 1

(putting her arms around GI 1)

Oh my, how muscular you are.

(takes GI 1 to the front right of the stage and
they begin dancing)

GI 2

(to GAL 2, with a soft high pitched voice)

Hi.

GAL 2

(as she puts her arms around GI 2)

Oh my, how cute you are.

(takes GI 2 to the front left of the stage
and they begin dancing)

GI 4

(looking down, really nervous)

Uh.

GAL 4

(puts her arms around GI 4, smiles as she turns
and says to the audience)

I just adore the strong silent type.

(She starts dancing with GI 4 in the front center of the stage. "Rock around the Clock" ends. The four GI's and four gals go to the center of the stage and sing "Tell Me About Your New Plane" based on "Hello I Love You" written by Jim Morrison and performed by the Doors.)

GUYS

Hello, I love you
Won't you tell me your name

GALS

Hello, I love you
Tell me about your new plane

GUYS

Hello, I love you
Won't you tell me your name?

GALS

Hello, I love you
Tell me about your new plane

GUYS

She's walking down the street

GALS

How fast does it go, what's the top speed?

GUYS

Do you think you'll be the guy?

GALS

How high does it really fly?

GUYS

Hello, I love you
Won't you tell me your name?

GALS

Hello, I love you
Tell me about your new plane

GUYS

Hello, I love you
Won't you tell me your name?

GALS

Hello, I love you
Tell me about your new plane

GUYS

She holds her head so high

GALS

Can it drop bombs from the sky?

GUYS

Her arms are wicked, and her legs are long

GALS

What's it use for shielding, is it strong?

GUYS

Sidewalk crouches at her feet

GALS

Is the radar jammer hard to beat?

GUYS

Do you hope to make her see you, fool?

GALS

Does it use a special kind of fuel?

GUYS

Hello

GALS

Hello

GUYS

Hello

GALS

Hello

GUYS

Hello

GALS

Hello

GUYS

Hello

GUYS AND GALS

I want you
Hello
I need my baby

Hello
Hello
Hello
Hello
Hello
Hello
Hello
Hello

(The GI's and gals exit together on the right side of the stage. After they leave, Harvey and KGB Gal enter from the left side of the stage holding hands. They order a drink from the bar as the lights dim.)

Scene Six

Two weeks later in the KGB and CIA offices. The KGB office is on the left side of the stage and has a large Soviet flag, desk, and two chairs. The CIA office is on the right side of the stage and has a large American flag, desk, and two chairs. The lights are initially dim on the CIA side. On the KGB side, KGB 1 is sitting behind the desk, KGB GAL is sitting in a visitor chair, KGB 2 is standing.

KGB 1

(to KGB GAL)

It has now been two weeks since the gals have been seeing the Americans. How are things going with the GI's?

KGB GAL

(draws out "Hey")

They are all idiots! All they do is walk up to girls and say, "Hey". Do they really think that turns girls on?

KGB 2

I think he means, how are things going getting information on the U2 spy plane from the American GI's?

KGB GAL

(says "stupid" loudly)

Oh. Most of them are telling us very little. I think it is because they are stupid and don't know anything! But one of them is supplying lots of information.

KGB 2

I've sent the information to Moscow. Some of it matches well with information from other sources. Who is the person supplying the information and how are you getting the information? Seduction? Whisky?

KGB GAL

I wish I could say that it is my charm.

(flutters a Japanese fan)

But he is a strange one. He mentions a lot of ideological things.

KGB 1

Ideological? Hmm - do you think you could get him to defect?

KGB GAL

(slowly stands up, stretches her body, speaks
boastfully, draws out "any's")

I can get any guy…to do anything.

(The lights dim on the KGB side and brighten on the
CIA side. CIA 1 is sitting behind the desk, Harvey is
sitting in a visitor's chair, CIA 2 is standing)

CIA 1

Well Harvey, how is the misinformation campaign going?

HARVEY

Really well, sir. I passed on the information you gave me.

CIA 2

How about the ideological information?

HARVEY

Sir, I've been passing that on also. I think she is buying it.

CIA 1

Has she introduced you to anybody else, maybe some KGB agents?

HARVEY

She has mentioned that there are a couple of guys that she would like for me to meet.

CIA 2

(looks at CIA 1 who nods back)

Harvey, there is something that we would like to talk to you about. It would help your country immensely, but it would be a great sacrifice for you.

HARVEY

What, what is it sir? I'll do anything to serve my country.

CIA 1

Harvey, we would like for you to defect.

HARVEY

(surprised and shocked)

Defect? Why? I love my country.

CIA 2

The Soviets are starting to trust you. If you defect, we can continue to supply you with good information mixed with misinformation. They will like you more, promote you, and the next thing we know we will have someone in a high place in their country that can help our side.

HARVEY

But, but to defect, to leave America for good?

CIA 1

Son, it is for the good of your country, and what a land of opportunity it is. Just think, how many 18 year olds from Ft. Worth, Texas without a high school education get a chance to travel to the Soviet Union and serve their country? You are surely blessed.

HARVEY

(dreamily)

From Ft. Worth to Japan to the Soviet Union. Man, I really am a secret agent!

(The lights dim on the CIA side and brighten on the KGB side. We don't hear the conversation, but we can see that KGB 1, KGB 2, KGB GAL, and Harvey are talking and drinking in celebration. Everyone is smiling and laughing. Harvey is slapped on the back by the KGB agents and hugged by KGB Gal. The music starts as they dance and sing "Going to the USSR" based on "Back to the USSR" written by Paul McCartney and performed by The Beatles.)

KGB 1

Oh Moscow is where you...want to be

KGB GAL

Parties that go on all night

KGB 2

A rich culture and...his...to...ry

KGB GAL

The vodka is out of site!

KGB 1, KGB 2, and KGB GAL

You're going to the U.S.S.R.
You don't know how lucky you are boy
Going to the U.S.S.R.

KGB GAL

There's a club I know, I think you'll enjoy the place

KGB 1

Lots of neat fountains and domes

KGB 2

We're leaving tomorrow go and pack your case

KGB GAL

You're gonna feel right at home

KGB 1, KGB 2, and KGB GAL

You're going to the U.S.S.R.
You don't know how lucky you are boy
Going from the U.S., going from the U.S., going to the U.S.S.R.

KGB 1

Well the Ukraine girls really knock you out

KGB GAL

They leave the West behind

KGB 2

And Moscow girls make you sing and shout

KGB GAL

But Georgia's always on my, my, my, my, my, my mind

KGB 1, KGB 2, and KGB GAL

You're going to the U.S.S.R.

You don't know how lucky you are, boy
Going to the U.S.S.R.

KGB 1

Well the Ukraine girls really knock you out

KGB GAL

They leave the West behind

KGB 2

And Moscow girls make you sing and shout

KGB GAL

But Georgia's always on my, my, my, my, my, my mind

(KGB 1 and KGB 2 look amorously at
KGB Gal as they sing to her)

KGB 1

Show me round your snow peaked mountains way down south

KGB 2

Take me to your Daddy's farm

KGB 1

Let me hear you balalaikas ringing out

KGB 2

Come and keep your comrade warm

KGB 1, KGB 2, and KGB GAL

You're going to the U.S.S.R.
You don't know how lucky you are boy
Going to the U.S.S.R!

(lights dim)

Scene Seven

Six months later. The stage is split. On the left side is the KGB Colonel's office. There is a large Soviet flag on the wall, a desk, and three chairs. On the right side of the stage is a large sign that says "Minsk Radio Factory." Underneath it is a sign that says "Big Dance Tonight". Harvey is on the phone in a phone booth outside the factory on the front right of the stage. The right side of the stage is initially dark.

MARINA

(enthusiastically bursts into the KGB colonel's office
from the left side of stage, draws out second
syllable of "Hello")

Hello Uncle!

KGB COLONEL

Marina, how many times do I have to tell you that I have a very important position as a colonel in the KGB. You can't just burst in on me like that.

MARINA

(walking slowly over to him, draws out first syllable
of "sorry" and first syllable of "favorite")

I am sorry. Did I ever tell you that you are my favorite uncle?

KGB COLONEL

As far as I know, I am your only uncle. You have been living with me for
two years now, ever since your mother...well, you know. Anyway, you are
17 years old and it really is about time you got a job.

MARINA

(draws out first syllable of "Harvey")

I have a job now! I work at a pharmacy down the street from Harvey.
Anyway, I am here on official KGB business.

KGB COLONEL

And that would be?

MARINA

(draws out "big")

I think Harvey needs a big raise.

KGB COLONEL

First off, Harvey works for the factory and not for me and second, why does he need a raise?

MARINA

(draws out "me")

So he would have more money to spend on me, of course.

KGB COLONEL

Marina, you have only known him for a month. How do you know what kind of person he is?

MARINA

(draws out first syllable of "favorite" and "teeniest")

I, I just have a good feeling about him. And besides, I have this favorite uncle that is like a super important leader of the KGB and I am sure that he has run all kind of background checks the past six months on him and if there was anything, even the teeniest little bit wrong with him, you wouldn't let me get anywhere near him. Am I right?

KGB COLONEL

You are good. Remind me to consider you for a job in the interrogation department or the propaganda department. Are you seeing the American today?

MARINA

(draws out first syllable of "favorite")

My favorite American guy, as I like to call him. He is going with me to the factory dance this evening after work.

KGB COLONEL

Shouldn't you be at work right now?

MARINA

(draws out first syllable of "any")

I told them I would be late – official KGB business you know. And since they know about you, no one will give me any trouble.

KGB COLONEL

(draws out "and")

OK niece. I will consider your, uh, business. Now get back to work or I will have someone follow you today and tonight.

> (Marina smiles and scurries off. The lights dim in the KGB colonel's office and that side of the stage is cleared. The lights brighten on the right side of the stage where Harvey is talking on the phone to CIA 1 and CIA 2.)

HARVEY

Yes, I got the latest package of information and told them exactly what was in it...No, no signs of suspicion...Yes, I am still working in the factory – it has now been six months...Well, it is a bit dull...Actually, I am seeing someone... Her uncle is a KGB colonel...I figured you would like that... OK, I have to get back to work...Don't want anyone to miss me and start looking for me, it is almost quitting time here and there is a big factory dance tonight.

> (Harvey hangs up the phone and walks to the factory
> where he sees two coworkers wearing oversize blue
> jeans in tatters that keep slipping down)

FACTORY 1

Hey Harvey, there you are. We were getting ready to send out a search party.

HARVEY

Sorry guys, are we quitting early?

FACTORY 2

Have to Harvey, so we can get ready. Tonight is the big factory dance.

FACTORY 1

Hey Harvey, we're not the only ones looking for you. Some cute girl is trying to find you.

FACTORY 2

I told her that I was available, but she still wanted you.

(his tattered, oversize pants fall down)

HARVEY

(with a quizzical look)

Really, even with your, uh, high fashion?

FACTORY 2

Who knows, we could be trend setters. Someday people around the world may pay lots of money to look like us!

(The whistle blows and people gather for the dance on the left side
of the stage. On the back left of the stage the DJ is dressed in a
business suit with no tie. His open shirt collar is outside his suit.
He has a record player and a microphone that he puts on a table.)

MARINA

(walks in, sees Harvey, excitedly races over to him and
gives him a big hug, draws out first syllable of "favorite")

How's my favorite American guy?

HARVEY

(draws out first syllable of "favorite")

He's doing much better now that he is with his favorite Russian girl.

DJ

(speaking into the microphone)

Good evening my comrades. Ladies and gentlemen welcome to tonight's factory dance!

(applause)

As is the custom, we will start the evening with everyone's favorite – The Party Dance. Hit it!

> (The music starts and the performers dance and sing "Here Come the Commies" based on "Theme from The Monkees" by Tommy Boyce and Bobby Hart and performed by The Monkees. The dancers don't know how to "modern dance." Some try marching, others make crude dance moves. Several people trip and fall during the song.)

CAST

Here we come,

(snap fingers for the next three lines)

Walking down the street
We get respect from
Ev'ry one we meet

We're the Communist party
People say we're mighty and grand
We're always busy looking
To expand to some other land

(snap fingers for the next four lines)

We go wherever we want to
Do what we want to do
We'll start new revolutions
To make the world safe for you

(shout out)

AND THE KIDS!

We're the Communist party
People say we're mighty and grand
We're always busy looking
To expand to some other land

You'll find that we're friendly
Just do everything our way
We're the world leader
And we have got lots to say

(snap fingers for next three lines)

Any time, or anywhere,
Just look over your shoulder

(dancers look back over their shoulders at the dancers
behind them, smile and wave at them)

Guess who'll be standing there

We're the Communist party
People say we're mighty and grand
We're always busy looking
To expand to some other land

(there is a pile up in the middle of the stage as dancers collide and fall - they get up and start to dance,
bump into each other, and fall down again)

We're the Communist party
People say we're mighty and grand
We're always busy looking
To expand to some other land

You'll find that we're friendly
Just do everything our way
We're the world leader
And we have got lots to say

We're the Communist party!

(The lights dim on the stage and the spotlight shines
on Harvey and Marina who are holding hands by the
phone booth on the front right side of the stage)

HARVEY

Marina, I really like being with you.

MARINA

And I like being with you.

HARVEY

Shall we go inside and show them how to modern dance?

MARINA

Sure!

> (The stage lights brighten, the music starts, and the cast watches as Harvey and Mariana dance and sing "My Russian Girl" based on "Sugar Sugar" written by Andy Kim and Jeff Barry and performed by the Archies.)

HARVEY

Marina,
Oh, honey, honey
You are my Russian girl
And you got me wanting you

MARINA

Harvey,
Oh sugar, sugar
You are my American guy
And you got me wanting you

HARVEY

I just can't believe the loveliness of loving you

MARINA

I just can't believe it's true

HARVEY

I just can't believe the wonder of this feeling too

MARINA

I just can't believe it's true

HARVEY

Marina,
Oh, honey, honey
You are my Russian girl
And you got me wanting you

MARINA

Oh, Harvey
Oh, sugar, sugar
You are my American guy
And you got me wanting you

HARVEY

When I kissed you girl
I knew how sweet a kiss could be

MARINA

I know how sweet a kiss can be

HARVEY

Like the summer sunshine
Pour your sweetness over me

MARINA

Pour your sweetness over me

HARVEY

Oh pour little sugar on me honey
Pour a little sugar on me baby

MARINA

When you make love so sweet...yeah, yeah, yeah

HARVEY

Pour a little sugar on me...Oh yeah
Pour a little sugar on me honey
Pour a little sugar on me baby

MARINA

I'm gonna make love so sweet...hey, hey, hey

HARVEY

Pour a little sugar on me honey
Marina
Oh honey, honey
You are my Russian girl
And you got me wanting you
Oh...honey, honey

MARINA

Sugar, sugar

HARVEY

Honey, honey

MARINA

Sugar, sugar

HARVEY

You are my Russian girl

(Harvey and Marina embrace. A soldier marches in and
gives the DJ an envelope)

DJ

(Opens envelope, smiles, raises his fist in excitement
as he reads the message)

Attention my comrades. Ladies and gentlemen. It is my pleasure to an-
nounce this evening some wonderful news. The dreaded U2 spy plane
of the Imperialistic Americans has been shot down by our brave Soviet
warriors - the greatest fighting force the world has ever seen!

(The crowd claps and yells and people raise their
fists in excitement. At first Marina yells, waves both
hands over her head and jumps up and down. Harvey
doesn't yell, his hands are by his side. They look at
each other and then Harvey raises his fist and yells.
Marina is quiet and lowers both hands to her side.)

It is another fine example of the triumph of Communism over
Imperialism.

(lights dim)

Scene Eight

The next morning. Same set as the start of the previous scene. On the left side is the KGB Colonel's office. There is a large Soviet flag on the wall, a desk, and three chairs. On the right side of the stage is a large sign that says "Minsk Radio Factory." Underneath it, the "Big Dance Tonight" sign has been removed. Outside, on the front right side of the stage is a phone booth. Harvey is in the spotlight talking on the phone. CIA 1 and CIA 2 each have a phone and are in a second spotlight on the front far left side of the stage. The KGB Colonel's office on the left side of the stage is initially dark.

HARVEY

(frantically)

The, the U2 spy plane has been shot down! They, they have it in their possession! They will take it apart and analyze it. They will know that I have been giving them false information. The, the next thing I know they will be putting me in front of a firing squad - or worse! You, you have got to get me out of here, and it has to be real, real fast!

CIA 2

(calmly)

Harvey, Harvey. Get a grip man. Take a deep breath and relax. We deal with these situations all the time.

HARVEY

(slightly less frantic)

So...so what do I do?

CIA 1

(calmly)

Stay real calm and pretend that you think that everything you told them was true. Oh, you may have gotten some of the technical details mixed up, but that always happens. Just stay calm while we work through some of our other contacts.

(The lights dim on Harvey and CIA 1 and CIA 2 and
brighten in the KGB colonel's office)

KGB 1

Sir, with the U2 spy plane shot down, we no longer need Harvey.

KGB 2

And sir, with budget cuts and high unemployment, shouldn't we give Harvey's job to a fellow countryman?

KGB COLONEL

Hmm...So the question is what to do with Harvey? How good was the information he gave?

KGB 1

We are of course just now starting to analyze the U2 wreckage. Previously some of his information matched well with other sources.

KGB 2

But some of it was totally false. Do you think he was a CIA plant to pass along false information?

KGB COLONEL

Oh, I figured he was a CIA plant all along.

KGB 1

(surprised)

What? How, how did you know?

KGB COLONEL

We gave him a battery of technical tests and he flunked all of them. He only has a tenth grade education, but he was talking about technical details that only a PHD could understand.

KGB 2

So why did you keep him if you knew the information was false?

KGB COLONEL

Sometimes you can learn as much from the misinformation as you can from the real information.

KGB 1

So what's to become of Harvey?

KGB COLONEL

There is a complication - my niece is in love with him.

KGB 2

(shocked)

You? You are going to let family get in the way of doing your job?

KGB COLONEL

(loud and forcefully)

Of course not! I am going to let my family help me do my job!

KGB 1

(cautiously)

How is that sir?

KGB COLONEL

(calmly)

My niece is a modern girl. She will not fit well with our society here. She needs to go abroad. If Harvey goes back to the United States, he could take her with him.

KGB 2

But sir, why would the KGB High Council approve such a move? Returning a...returning a CIA spy?

KGB COLONEL

A CIA spy? Oh no, no, no. He is not a CIA spy. He is spying for Mother Russia. A double spy. He is pretending to work for the CIA but he is really working for us. And with Marina with him, we will always be able to track him.

(pauses, gives a stern stare, speaks slowly and loudly)

Are we clear on this gentlemen?

KGB 1

(flattering)

A brilliant idea sir! But will Harvey take your niece with him?

KGB COLONEL

(sternly, slow and loud)

He will if we tell him that the only way for him to leave the country alive is to marry my niece.

KGB 2

But sir, what if Harvey dumps your niece once he gets to America?

KGB COLONEL

(puts his arms around KGB 1 and KGB 2 and walks
them to the front center of the stage)

Over the years, many fathers have threatened harm to young men if they ever broke their daughter's heart - but how many of them have had the power of the KGB to back up the threat!

(The lights dim. The spotlight focuses on Harvey and Marina at the front of the stage wearing cowboy hats and singing "We're   Going to Texas" based on "Deep in the Heart of Texas" by June Hershey and Don Swander. After the first few stanzas, the stage brightens and the cast, wearing cowboy hats, joins the singing and country western dancing. The audience is motioned to join in the singing of the chorus. XXXX denotes clapping.)

HARVEY

(to Marina)

The stars at night
Are big and bright XXXX
Deep in the heart of Texas

MARINA

(to Harvey)

Reminds me of
The one I love XXXX
Deep in the heart of Texas

HARVEY

(to Marina)

The prairie sky
Is wide and high XXXX
Deep in the heart of Texas

MARINA

(to Harvey)

If I'm with you
I'll never be blue XXXX
Deep in the heart of Texas

(lights brighten, cast is on stage)

CIA 1 and CIA 2

Be aware
Thing are going on there XXXX

CAST

Deep in the heart of Texas

KGB COLONEL

Military bases
Top secret places XXXX

CAST and AUDIENCE

(Cast motions for audience to join in the singing of the chorus)

Deep in the heart of Texas

KGB 1 and KGB 2

The new space race
Is taking place XXXX

CAST and AUDIENCE

Deep in the heart of Texas

CUBA 1 AND CUBA 2

Cuban cigars
And big fancy cars XXXX

CAST and AUDIENCE

Deep in the heart of Texas

FBI 1 and FBI 2

The state's crime free
It's safe as can be XXXX

CAST and AUDIENCE

Deep in the heart of Texas

MAFIA 1 and MAFIA 2

For a bang-up job
Come join our mob XXXX

CAST and AUDIENCE

Deep in the heart of Texas

JACK

For a real good time
See this club of mine XXXX

CAST and AUDIENCE

Deep in the heart of Texas

A

You'll do great
In the Lone Star State XXXX

CAST and AUDIENCE

Deep in the heart of Texas

G

Rich billionaires
Shape world affairs

CAST and AUDIENCE

Deep in the heart of Texas

DETECTIVE

Be their star
And you'll go far XXXX

CAST and AUDIENCE

Deep in the heart of Texas

F

The political machine
Is not real clean XXXX

CAST and AUDIENCE

Deep in the heart of Texas

CAST

There are hidden things
Behind the scenes

(progressively louder)

Deep in the heart, Deep in the heart, DEEP IN THE HEART

HARVEY and MARINA

(loud and excited)

We're going to...

CAST

(very loud)

TEXAS!

(lights dim)

Scene Nine

Three years later. Harvey and Mariana are sitting in their living room in Irving, Texas. It is very plain - there is a table, two chairs, a TV, and a playpen. Harvey is sitting in a chair watching TV. The front door is on the left side of the stage, the back door is on the right side of the stage.

MARINA

(walks over to Harvey and gives him a hug, draws out
first syllable of "favorite")

Did I ever tell you that you are my favorite American guy?

HARVEY

(without looking up from watching TV)

Yes. Yes dear.

MARINA

(draws out first syllable of "favorite")

And what about me? After three years of marriage am I still you're favorite Russian girl?

HARVEY

(focused on the TV)

Yes. Yes dear.

MARINA

(draws out first syllable of "favorite")

And what about our one year old daughter June, is she your favorite
Texas kid?

HARVEY

(still focused on the TV)

Yes. Yes dear.

MARINA

(annoyed, draws out "right")

And would it be ok if I got a gun and shot you right now?

(makes her hand into the shape of a gun and fires it
three times into Harvey's left side)

HARVEY

(doesn't look up from watching the TV)

Yes. Yes dear.

MARINA

(loud and angry, draws out first syllable of
"Harvey", "now", and "me")

Harvey! Get up out of the chair right now and listen to me!

(There is a knock at the front door)

HARVEY

(calmly)

Just, just a minute dear.

(Harvey goes to the front door and takes a stuffed
legal envelope from CIA 1)

CIA 1

Here are the pictures for you Harvey.

We'll have some more next week.

(they leave)

MARINA

Harvey, why do strange people show up here all the time giving you packages? I thought you worked in a printing office.

HARVEY

I do. We print publications for Congress and government agencies.

MARINA

So why do they bring the pictures here?

HARVEY

(shrugs his shoulders)

Oh, I don't know. Some of the information is top secret, maybe they don't want it to fall into the wrong hands.

(They are interrupted by knocking at the back door.
Harvey opens the door.)

KGB 1

Harvey, do you have a package for us?

HARVEY

Sure do. Here it is.

(hands the package he just received from CIA 1 to KGB 1)

KGB 2

We'll see you next week.

(the KGB agents leave)

MARINA

(initially has a puzzled look but shrugs it off, draws out
first syllable of "Harvey" and "really")

Anyway, Harvey. I need to talk to you about something really important -
and top secret!

(excitedly)

I think we should have another baby!

HARVEY

(with a shocked look stumbles into his chair, speaks
slowly and noncommittally)

Well...well...well...that is certainly a possibility.

TV ANNOUNCER

We interrupt this program for some important breaking news. An invasion of Cuba will be starting in a few hours. Cuban exiles will be attacking Cuba near the Bay of Pigs. We will keep you informed. Now back to our regularly scheduled program in progress.

MARINA

(draws out first syllable in Harvey)

Well Harvey, what do you think?

HARVEY

(loudly)

That has got to be the stupidest thing I have ever heard!

MARINA

(shocked, with a disappointed look)

What?

HARVEY

They are announcing an invasion before it takes place! The Cubans will be waiting for them at the Bay of Pigs. The invasion is doomed to fail.

MARINA

(greatly relieved, draws out "nice")

Oh that's awful dear. Now as I was saying, a second Texas baby sure would be nice.

(They are interrupted by knocking at the front door.
Harvey opens the front door and sees the two CIA agents)

HARVEY

What, why are you guys here? I thought you weren't coming back until next week.

CIA 1

Harvey, we need to transfer you to a new city.

CIA 2

(looking over at Mariana)

Yes. It is very important for our, uh, business. And it is a great advancement opportunity for you.

HARVEY

Well, where to?

CIA 1

There is a place in New Orleans.

HARVEY

But, what about the printing press? Who will do my, uh, job here?

CIA 2

We will have to find someone else, but right now, New Orleans is the hot spot for our, uh, business.

(CIA 1 and CIA 2 leave)

HARVEY

Marina, we may need to move to...

(They are interrupted by knocking at the back door. Harvey opens the back door and sees the two KGB agents)

HARVEY

What, why are you guys here? You said you weren't coming back until next week.

KGB 1

Harvey, we need to transfer you to a new city.

HARVEY

(nervously)

A new city, but I...where?

KGB 2

We need you to go to New Orleans.

HARVEY

(relieved)

Oh sure.

(KGB 1 and KGB 2 leave)

MARINA

(sternly with a confrontational look)

Move to New Orleans?

HARVEY

Well, I am only thinking about you and the kid.

MARINA

(loud and in disbelief)

What?

HARVEY

You know...You always said you wanted to see more of America and this is a good opportunity for me to make some more money to buy nice things for you and the kid.

MARINA

(sternly)

On one condition.

HARVEY

Anything, anything you want.

MARINA

(excitedly)

A second kid!

(The lights dim. The Troubadour, dressed as a spy wearing a trench coat with dark glasses appears in the spotlight on the front right of the stage and sings "House Where Evil Deeds are Done" based on "House of the Rising Sun" as performed by The Animals.)

TROUBADOUR

There is a house in New Orleans
Where evil deeds are done
And it's been the ruin of many a poor boy
And God I know I'm one

My father was an exporter
Mom was a buccaneer
I became a double spy
We always lived with fear

Now spying is a dangerous game
You move around a lot
Cover your tracks and watch your back
It's so easy to get caught

(pulls out a handgun, looks back over his shoulder, and cautiously walks around stage trying to avoid capture)

Oh mother tell your children
Go out and have lots of fun
Don't spend your lives in sin and misery
Helping evil deeds to be done

There once was a man who thought he could
Spy for three or four or five
To obtain fame can be insane
How could he stay alive?

Well there is a house in New Orleans
Where evil deeds are done
And its been the ruin of many a poor boy
And God I know I'm one.

(lights dim)

Scene Ten

A few weeks later at "The House Where Evil Deeds Are Done" in New Orleans. There are five identical offices. Each has one desk, two chairs, a phone, and a large sign. The first office sign from the left side of the stage is "CIA Transport", the second office sign is "Cuban Cigars", the third office sign is "Mobs -R- Us", the fourth office sign is "FBI", and the fifth office sign is "KGB Vodka". There are two people in each office talking on the phone, taking notes, etc. As Harvey enters the stage from the left, he sees three odd looking men in blue jeans with white tee shirts that have a single red letter on the front and back. The first has the letter "F", the second has the letter "G", and the third has the letter "A". Harvey is also wearing blue jeans and a white tee shirt. The three men act quirky - they walk in circles skip, and jump. They prance as they talk to Harvey.

F

Hi, Harvey. Welcome to New Orleans.

HARVEY

(looking puzzled)

How, how do you know my name? And why are you…

G

Oh we know a lot about you.

A

We know lots about lots of people.

F

We've been around for a long, long time.

G

And we'll be around for a long, long time to come.

(Harvey gives them another puzzled look)

A

The people you want to see are inside.

(Harvey enters the second office with the "Cuban
Cigars" sign. Cuba 1 and Cuba 2 are in the office.
They are dressed in tropical shirts and shorts. They
are wearing straw hats and have cigars in their
hands. They speak with fake Spanish accents. When
Harvey arrives, they quickly put away papers that
were on the desk.)

CUBA 1

Welcome, Harvey. Sit down.

(pulls out chair for him)

HARVEY

Thank you.

CUBA 2

We have some, uh, friends that said you were a good source of information.

HARVEY

Yes…I saw on television what happened at the Bay of Pigs, and I would like to help you.

CUBA 1

Excuse me. Harvey, you are a gringo. Why would you help us? Why would you want to work against your country?

HARVEY

My country? Oh no, don't get me wrong. It isn't my country that is the enemy. It is the Mafia. They desecrated your beautiful country with casinos and illegal activities. When you kicked them out, they launched the Bay of Pigs invasion.

CUBA 2

So why are you coming forth now?

HARVEY

I have a young child. Do you have any children?

CUBA 1

Si, I have four children.

CUBA 2

And maybe a lot more he doesn't know about!

HARVEY

Anyway, I want my child to grow up in a world that is safe, and I think you will agree that it is important that we save the kids.

CUBA 1

(loudly)

Save the kids!

CUBA 2

(loudly)

Viva Castro and viva the kids!

CUBA 1

That sounds good. Now Harvey, what we really need for you to do is make friends with the Mafia. Like you say, they are the ones that invaded us. We need you to infiltrate them and give them information about our defenses in case they attack again.

HARVEY

Information that they can use to attack you?

CUBA 2

It is false information! Lies! Surely you gringos have heard of misinformation. Take this package and go see the Mafia.

(Harvey takes the information, leaves, and goes to the "Mobs-R-Us" office next door. Mafia 1 and Mafia 2 are in the office. They are dressed in black pants and long sleeve pullover black shirts and are wearing black hats. They speak with fake Italian accents. There are two guns on the desk. After Harvey arrives, they discreetly put the guns away.)

HARVEY

Hello, my name is Harvey. Do you work for the Mafia?

MAFIA 1

Mafia? Who us? Oh no, no, no.

(points to the Mobs-R-Us sign)

We are respectable businessmen.

HARVEY

Oh, I am sorry. I have a package of information on Cuban defenses that I would like to sell to the Mafia, but if that's not you…

MAFIA 2

(draws out "well")

Well, hold on there Harvey…

(looking at Mafia 1 who nods back)

We, of course, are not members of any Mafia, but what's in the package?

(They open the package, look through it, and nod)

MAFIA 1

Like we said, we are not members of the Mafia, but this information could be useful to some friends of ours.

MAFIA 2

Some good American friends!

MAFIA 1

How did you get this information and can you get more?

HARVEY

Sure. I have some friends in Cuba that are really upset at the Castro regime. They are hoping that he will be overthrown, so they are trying to get this information in the hands of people that might launch another invasion.

MAFIA 2

But why would you want to help us?

HARVEY

I have a young child. Do you have any children?

MAFIA 1

Yes, I have several and I love them all dearly.

HARVEY

(looking at Mafia 2)

And you?

MAFIA 2

Oh yes. We have the same godfather and he visits us often.

HARVEY

Well then, you know what it is like. I want my children to grow up in a safe America. We don't need an ugly cancer like Castro at our door step. I will do anything to help make the world safer for kids.

MAFIA 1

(loudly)

Save the kids!

MAFIA 2

(loudly)

Yes, save the kids!

MAFIA 1

Harvey, we certainly appreciate your information, and look forward to working with you in the future. Would you be able to pass on some information?

HARVEY

Who me? Well I guess so. What do you want to pass on and to whom does it go?

MAFIA 2

Harvey, as you know we are respectable businessmen.

HARVEY

Of course.

MAFIA 1

From time to time we discover that our, uh, competitors have broken the law.

MAFIA 2

And we would like to pass that information to the FBI.

HARVEY

Sure, but why do you need me?

MAFIA 1

Let's just say it's not good for business if we talk directly to the FBI.

MAFIA 2

We need a middleman. Usually we like to use people like Marilyn Monroe, but under the circumstances...

MAFIA 1

So would you be willing, as a good friend, to take this information to the FBI?

> (Harvey takes the package, leaves, and walks to the
> FBI office next door. FBI 1 and FBI 2 are sitting in
> the office. They are dressed in blue suits with white
> shirts and narrow black ties. They are very nerdy. As
> Harvey walks in, FBI 1 has just pointed out some-
> thing on some paperwork to FBI 2 and is chuckling.
> FBI 2 sees it and slaps his knee while laughing.)

HARVEY

(initially with a puzzled look)

Hello, my name is Harvey and I have some information that you may find useful.

FBI 1

Well let's see...

(takes the info from Harvey while still laughing)

What do you have here?

(FBI 1 and FBI 2 look over the papers)

FBI 2

(draws out "very")

Hmm…interesting, very interesting. How did you get this information?

HARVEY

Let's just say I have a friend that got caught up with the Mafia. He wants to get out, but if he comes directly to you, they will hunt him down, so he gave me the information.

FBI 1

Can he get more information?

HARVEY

I am sure he can.

FBI 2

So what's in it for you?

HARVEY

I have a young child. Do you have any children?

FBI 1

Oh yes. A boy. I started him watching cops and robbers shows on TV at a young age so he will grow up to be just like me.

FBI 2

I'm Sergeant Friday. Just the facts Ma'am.

(FBI 1 and FBI 2 laugh and slap their knees.
Harvey gives them a puzzled look)

HARVEY

Well, as I watch my child grow up, I realize that children need to live in a better world. We need to get rid of evil and make the world safe for the kids.

FBI 1

(loudly)

Yes, make the world safe for kids!

FBI 2

(loudly)

Save the kids!

FBI 1

Harvey, you could be a good middleman.

HARVEY

What, what do you mean?

FBI 2

We have some, uh, information that we need to pass on to certain parties that is very sensitive.

HARVEY

Why don't you just give it to them?

FBI 1

Let's just say that we can't be seen with them, we need a good middleman.

HARVEY

Well, OK. Where do I take the information?

FBI 2

To the KGB and to the, uh, CIA.

> (The lights dim as the stage is cleared. The spotlight shines on Harvey, F, G, and A in the front center of the stage. F, G, and A are initially walking in circles.)

F

How's it going Harvey?

G

Got things figured out?

A

A bit confused?

HARVEY

Huh, how do, how do you know?

(F, G, and A start skipping)

F

Oh, we know a lot about a lot of things.

G

We've been around for a long, long time.

A

And we'll be around for a long, long time to come.

(F, G, and A stop skipping and walk over to Harvey)

F

Let's see if we have things straight.

G

You are working for the CIA by providing false information to the KGB and by infiltrating the Castro Cuban regime.

A

You are getting paid by the KGB for obtaining the information given to you by the CIA.

F

You are working for the Castro Cuban regime by giving false information to the Mafia.

G

You are working for the Mafia by giving the FBI information on rival gangs in exchange for leniency on Mafia operations.

A

And you are working for the FBI by being their middleman with the KGB and the CIA, who is their real enemy because they compete for limited government funding.

F

You are a secret agent for five different groups!

G

Think of the opportunities to advance! Think of the opportunities to make money!

A

You are the top spy in the land!

F

Don't you find the whole thing a bit frightening?

(The music starts to "The Spinning Wheel Guy" based on "Spinning Wheel" written by David Clayton-Thomas and performed by Blood, Sweat, and Tears. Five groups - CIA 1 and CIA 2, KGB 1 and KGB 2, CUBA 1 and CUBA 2, MAFIA 1 and MAFIA 2, and FBI 1 and FBI 2 are standing in a semicircle in the center of the stage. Mariana is in the middle of the semicircle. F, G, and A are standing next to a spinning wheel on the front right side of the stage and spin the spinning wheel and prance around each time the song mentions "spinning wheel". During the song, Harvey spins between the five groups. When he comes to one group, Marina goes to that group and tries to grab him, but they "spin" Harvey to the next group just before she can reach him. Mariana then goes to the next group and almost grabs him before he is spun to the next group, etc. Three signs are posted on the front of the stage - "Love and Happiness" points to the left, "Fame and Fortune" point to the right, and "Success" points both ways. Cast members watch the spinning and carry additional signs for their causes.)

CAST

What goes up, must come down
Spinning wheel got to go round
You get to fix the troubles it's a crying sin
Ride a painted pony
Let the spinning wheel spin
We got no money - you have lots of hope
Spinning wheel's all alone
You get to fix the troubles, and you'll really learn
Ride a painted pony
Let the spinning wheel turn

(Cast members raise their signs and march around stage. CIA 1, CIA 2, KGB 1, KGB 2, CUBA 1, and CUBA 2 raise their country's flags, FBI 1 and FBI 2 raise signs with the scales of justice symbol, MAFIA 1 and MAFIA 2 raise signs with the money symbol)

Did you find a directing sign
On life's straight and narrow highway?
Would you mind a reflecting sign
Just let us get inside your mind
And show you the causes that are real

(Harvey is spun between the various groups. Mariana tries to catch him, but barely misses)

Someone is waiting just for you
Spinning wheel is spinning true
Drop all your troubles, go be by her side
Catch a painted pony
On the spinning wheel ride

(Harvey is spun between the various groups.
Mariana tries to catch him, but barely misses)

Someone is waiting just for you
Spinning wheel is spinning true
Drop all your troubles, go be by her side
Ride a painted pony
You're the spinning wheel guy!

(Harvey is spun between the various groups
Mariana tries to catch him, but barely misses)

MARINA

(finally grabs Harvey after the song ends)

Harvey, this is crazy! You have a wife and a small kid at home, but you are always away at work. You need to come home and spend time with your family. Why are you doing this?

HARVEY

But, but Mariana, I am doing this for my family. I am doing this for you.

MARINA

(loud and incredulous, draws out "me" and "way")

For me? Oh no, no, no, no. No way!...It's not for me! I am the one that wants you home!

HARVEY

Then I am doing it for the kids. For our kid and all the kids in the world.
I am making the world a better place for all of them.

(looks over at the people from the five offices)

Hey guys, why do you do what you do?

CIA 1 and CIA 2

Oh, it's for the kids.

KGB 1 and KGB 2

Definitely for the kids.

CUBA 1 and CUBA 2

Viva Castro and the kids!

MAFIA 1 and MAFIA 2

For the kids! They are our future customers.

FBI 1 and FBI 2

It's the kids. Every kid needs to feel safe.

(The music starts to "For the Kids" based on "For Your Love" written by Graham Gouldman and performed by The Yardbirds. Some of

the cast members carry posters with pictures of kids. When the song mentions "kill anything in sight", cast members grab an assortment of weapons and aim at each other. Mariana is furious and paces back and forth with her arms folded.)

CAST

For the Kids

For the Kids

For the Kids
I'll give them everything and more, and that's for sure
For the Kids
I'll bring them Barbie dolls and go karts to their door

For the Kids
I will use all my might
And take on any fight

(weapons out and aimed at each other)

I'll kill anything in sight
So they can sleep safe at night

(next three "Kids" are drawn out)

For the Kids
For the Kids
For the Kids

For the Kids, for the Kids
I will give the stars above
For the Kids, for the Kids

I will give them all I can

For the Kids

For the Kids

For the Kids
I'd give the moon if it were mine to give
For the Kids
I'd give the stars and the sun 'fore I live
For the Kids
I will use all my might
And take on any fight

(weapons out and aimed at each other)

I'll kill anything in sight
So they can sleep safe at night

(next four "Kids" are drawn out)

For the Kids
For the Kids
For the Kids
For the Kids

MARINA

(increasingly loud and angry)

For the kids! For the Kids! FOR THE KIDS! You Have Got To Be
KIDDING!!!

(The music starts for "It's Not For The Kids" based on "Can't Buy Me Love" written by Paul McCartney and performed by The Beatles. First three "Kids" are drawn out.)

It's for the kids, no

                              (shakes head)

Kids no

                              (shakes head)

It's for the kids, no

                              (shakes head)

You say you want to go to war, so your kids will be safe at night
Arm your soldiers, make battle plans, give them quite a fight
But your kids don't care a-bout the war, they want you home at night

You say that you are working late, so your kids will have things new
You go on trips make lots of money, that is what you do
But your kids don't care a-bout the money, they want to spend time with you

                        (next two "kids" are drawn out)

It's for the kids, everybody tells me so

                  (fires gun finger four times on "no, no, no, no")

It's for the kids, no, no, no, no!

You say that you are helping make - the world a better place
And I think that it is really grand, to save the human race
But your kids don't care a-bout the world, they want to see your face.

(screams and pulls out her hair, next two "kids"
are drawn out)

It's for the kids, everybody tells me so

(fires gun finger four times on "no, no, no, no")

It's for the kids, no, no, no, no!

Spend more time with your kids, they need you every day
Go places with them, talk to them, hear what they have to say
Growing up is - not easy, help them find their way.

It's for your kids, yes
For your kids, yes
It's for your kids right now.

(The curtain closes ending Act 1)

ACT 2

Scene One

The lights dim, the curtain opens and the video screen displays a montage of pictures of various hands. The hands are of different sizes, shapes, colors, and ages. The Troubadour and dancers appear and the music starts to "Hidden Hands" based on "Rock On" written and performed by David Essex. The video screen is turned off, leaving the stage in total darkness. Black lights at the front of the stage are then turned on, so only objects that glow in the black lights are visible to the audience.

The Troubadour is wearing dark clothes with oversized white gloves and glow-in-the-dark lipstick, so the audience only sees gloves and lips. Dancers dressed in dark clothes with oversized white gloves pass in front of the black lights, so the audience only sees hands that appear to float in midair. Other dancers are dressed in black and carry dark sacks that contain objects that glow in the black lights. They pull the objects from the sacks and put them back into the sacks, giving the audience the impression that these objects have somehow magically appeared out of thin air and then disappeared.

For the second verse, the dancers go to the back of the stage and the video screen is turned on displaying pictures of people working with their hands. There are pictures of people working in factory assembly lines, construction workers with tools in their hands, soldiers with guns in their hands, etc. The video screen then shows some of the greatest accomplishments made by hands. Pictures are shown of the Pyramids, Great Wall of China, Taj Mahal, Eiffel Tower, Empire State

Building, a battleship, an offshore drilling rig, and the space shuttle. Interspersed are pictures of the different individual hands shown at the beginning of the scene. The montage ends with a picture of the World Trade Center on fire and the Troubadour singing "Oh no."

DANCERS

(drawn out)

Ooh

TROUBADOUR

Before time began
There were - hidden hands
Have you seen them work, have you?

Hidden hands behind the scenes
Come together to make others dreams
Creating fortunes, crowning kings — never seen

And where do they go from here?
What will they make appear?

So many great improvements they can make
Sorrow and miseries they create
Who controls the hidden hands, do you?

DANCERS

Hidden hands

TROUBADOUR

And where do they go from here?
What will they make appear?
So many great improvements they can make

TROUBADOUR and DANCERS

Sorrow and miseries they create

TROUBADOUR

(points to various sections of the audience
during "Do you?")

Who controls the hidden hands, do you?

Do you?
Do you?
Do you?
Who controls the hidden hands?
Do you?
Who controls the hidden hands?
Do you?
Who controls the hidden hands?
Do you?
Who controls the hidden hands?
Do you?
Who controls the hidden hands?
Do you?
Who controls the hidden hands?
Do you?

Who controls the hidden hands?
Do you?
Who controls the hidden hands?
Do you?

(dancers go to back of stage and video screen is turned on)

DANCERS

(draw out "Ooo")

Ooo

TROUBADOUR

Before time began
There were - hidden hands
Have you seen them work, have you?

Hidden hands behind the scenes
Come together to make others dreams
Creating fortunes, crowning kings — never seen.

And where do they go from here?
What will they make appear?
So many great improvements they can make
Sorrows and miseries they create
Who controls the hidden hands, do you?

DANCERS

Hidden hands

TROUBADOUR

And where do they go from here?
What will they make appear?
So many great improvements they can make

TROUBADOUR and DANCERS

Sorrow and miseries they create

TROUBADOUR

Who controls the hidden hands, do you?

Oh no!
Oh no!
Oh no!
Hey there hidden hands
Oh no!
Hey there hidden hands
Oh no!
Hey there hidden hands
Oh no!
Hey there hidden hands
Oh no!
Hey there hidden hands
Oh no!
Hey there hidden hands
Oh no!
Hey there hidden hands
Oh no!
Hey there hidden hands
Oh no!
Hey there hidden hands
Oh no!

Scene Two

Harvey and Marina are at home watching TV. Mariana is pregnant and is wearing a maternity dress. Their home is sparse - a TV, two chairs, and a table. There is a doll on the table. The front door is on the left side of the stage.

NARRATOR

The time is one year later. The world is filled with fear. The Soviet Union is installing missiles in Cuba that could be used to attack the United States. World War III could begin at any moment. Harvey and Marina are in their apartment in New Orleans.

MARINA

(comes up behind Harvey who is sitting in a chair watching TV and gives him a big hug, draws out first syllable of "favorite")

Did my favorite American guy make the news today?

HARVEY

Oh. You are talking, talking about last week. That was, uh, just for pub-
licity to show the company I work for how dedicated I am.

MARINA

(teasingly with a big smile, draws out "what")

And what is the name of that company?

HARVEY

Well, uh, they don't really have a name. It is just a group of guys that
work together.

TV ANNOUNCER

We interrupt this program with some breaking news. Evidence has come
forth this evening that the Soviets are building missile silos in Cuba.
Missiles launched from these silos could reach much of the southern
United States. Here are U2 spy plane photos that show...

(There is a loud knock on the front door. Harvey
opens the door and CIA 1 and CIA 2 enter)

HARVEY

What, what are you guys doing here?

CIA 1

Harvey, something very important has just come up. We need you to go....

(looks over and sees Marina)

Uh, go on a business trip for us.

HARVEY

Sure, where am I going?

CIA 2

To Cuba.

HARVEY

(looks startled, points at the TV)

I, I just saw on the news that Cuba...

CIA 1

Yes, yes. We need to get a, uh, package delivered to Cuba.

HARVEY

OK, so how do I get there?

CIA 2

Well, as you know, there are no longer any direct flights between the United States and Cuba. But there are flights between Mexico City and Cuba.

CIA 1

We need you to drive to Mexico City and obtain a special pass that will allow you to fly from Mexico City to Cuba.

CIA 2

We'll see you in Mexico City.

(CIA 1 and CIA 2 leave)

MARINA

Harvey?

HARVEY

Yes Marina.

MARINA

Do you ever get lonely on your business trips?

HARVEY

Lonely?

MARINA

Yes, lonely. I really miss you when you are away. When you are gone, I am here all by myself taking care of our kid and I feel so lonely. I really don't want to be alone.

HARVEY

We live on a planet full of sad, lonely people.

MARINA

Did you get that out of one of your books?

HARVEY

We live in a society because of our fear of loneliness. People will do all kinds of jobs, some that are horrible, just to be accepted by others so they won't feel so lonely.

MARINA

I look around and see happy, busy people doing things they enjoy - but at times I am lonely. Very lonely. Are you saying that everyone gets lonely?

HARVEY

If you look deep enough, you can see loneliness everywhere. Painful loneliness. People that hurt because they are lonely. Here, I'll show you.

(The music starts to "It's a Lonely World" based on "Eleanor Rigby" written by Paul McCartney and John Lennon and performed by The Beatles. In the back of the stage are various scenes of loneliness - a person at work sitting at a desk watching the clock, an old woman eating slowly by herself, Jack sitting in a chair petting his black cat, an old man whittling, and a soldier holding a gun on guard duty.)

HARVEY

Ah, look at all the lonely people
Ah, look at all the lonely people
Man was created
And felt the unbearable pain of being alone

MARINA

God gave him Eve

HARVEY

Was she so lonely
That she talked to a snake so she had something to do?

MARINA

(singing into a bathrobe belt shaped like a snake)

You might have too

HARVEY and MARINA

(pointing to the lonely people at the back of the stage)

All the lonely people
Where do they all come from?
All the lonely people
Where do they all belong?

HARVEY

Billions of people
Filling their days with the meaningless tasks that they learn

MARINA

Where does one turn?

HARVEY

Looking for leaders
To give them a name or a cause that is worthy to claim

MARINA

It's really a shame

HARVEY and MARINA

All the lonely people
Where do they all come from?
All the lonely people
Where do they all belong?

HARVEY

Ah, look at all the lonely people
Ah, look at all the lonely people

All the hard workers
Building monuments grand where they can 'cross the land

MARINA

That turn into sand

HARVEY

All the great warriors
Gallantly die for the cause of their faraway king

MARINA

What did it mean?

HARVEY and MARINA

All the lonely people
Where do they all come from?
All the lonely people
Where do they all belong?

(lights dim)

Scene Three

Offices at the Mexico City Airport a few days later. A large "Mexico City Airport" banner is hung at the back of the stage. There are five offices, each with a desk, two chairs, and a large company sign. The signs in the offices from left to right are "CIA Transport", "Come C Cuba", "Mobs-R-Us", "Fried Beans Inc.," and "Soviet Travel" On the far right front side of the stage is a reception area with a TV and chair. There are people in the offices talking on the phone, working on papers, etc.

HARVEY

(walks into the first office on the far left of the stage
which has a "CIA TRANSPORT" sign)

Hello, do you have my special pass?

CIA 1

Harvey, there has been a delay. We have contacted someone very high up. We are waiting for a response, but it may take some time.

It is very important for your country that you get to Cuba. You may want to try other channels.

HARVEY

(leaves the office and walks to the office next door.
He stops, reads the sign "Come C Cuba", sees the
female clerk, and enters)

Hello, my name is Harvey and I would like to get a special pass to travel to Cuba.

COME C CUBA CLERK

(doesn't look up from her paperwork, has a
bored monotone voice)

Fill out these forms.

HARVEY

I have some friends in the cigar business. Here is a card they gave me.

(hands card from wallet to clerk)

COME C CUBA CLERK

Let's see.

(abruptly stands at attention and
is very accommodating)

Cuban Cigars? Yes sir! Of course. Let me make some phone calls. Would you mind waiting? It may take a few minutes. There is a reception area outside.

HARVEY

(leaves the office and walks next door, stops, and reads the
"Mobs-R-Us" sign, sees a worker, and enters the office)

Hey, I have worked with your company before. I met a couple of your associates in New Orleans. Here, I have one of their business cards.

(hands him a business card from his wallet)

MOBS-R-US AGENT

(takes the card and abruptly stands at attention,
speaks with a fake Italian accent)

Our, uh, company is very close knit. It is like one big family. A friend of an associate is a friend of mine. What are you doing in Mexico?

HARVEY

I am trying to get a special pass to travel to Cuba.

MOBS-R-US AGENT

(looks incredulous, laughs)

A special pass? We go there all the time. You don't need a special pass. Do you want a ride?

HARVEY

Sure, when do we leave?

MOBS-R-US AGENT

Let me make some calls. It may be a few minutes. There is a waiting room outside.

HARVEY

(leaves the office and walks to the office next door,
stops and reads the "Fried Beans Inc" sign, then
recognizes the people inside)

Hey, I know you guys. You are with the FBI.

(Startled, the agents put their fingers to their lips to
hush Harvey. Harvey looks at the sign again)

Oh, I get it. Fried Beans Inc...F-B-I. What are you doing here? I thought you guys only worked in the USA.

FBI 1

Sometimes the boundaries of the United States are, uh, extended.

FBI 2

And sometimes we, uh, go on vacation. What brings you here?

HARVEY

I am trying to get to Cuba on some, uh, business.

FBI 1

We have some special connections. We'll give them a call.

FBI 2

It may be a few minutes. You can wait outside.

HARVEY

(leaves the office and walks to the office next door,
stops and reads the "Soviet Travel" sign, sees the
female travel agent, and walks inside)

Greetings comrade. I used to live in the Soviet Union. In fact, I married
a fine Russian girl.

SOVIET TRAVEL AGENT

That's great comrade. What brings you here?

HARVEY

I am trying to get a special pass to travel to Cuba.

SOVIET TRAVEL AGENT

(with a questioning look)

An American going to Cuba in the middle of an international crisis?

HARVEY

Here is my special friend of the Soviet Union card.

(takes out card and hands it to the agent)

SOVIET TRAVEL AGENT

(takes the card, looks at it, and then abruptly
stands at attention)

KGB Vodka? Yes, of course comrade. Let me make some calls. You can
wait outside.

HARVEY

Sure. I'll come back later.

(walks to the reception area, sits down,
and watches TV)

TV ANNOUNCER

We interrupt this program to bring breaking news. The Cuban missile crisis is over. Repeat. The Cuban missile crisis is over. The Soviet Union has bowed to the demands of the US president and has agreed to withdraw its missiles from Cuba, thereby preventing the outbreak of World War III. Repeating. The Cuban missile crisis is over.

(The phones in all of the offices ring. The people in the offices
answer the phone, nod, and hang up.)

HARVEY

(walks back to the Soviet Travel office)

Have you heard any more?

SOVIET TRAVEL AGENT

(rips up Harvey's card)

You are no longer a special friend of the Soviet Union.

HARVEY

(with a startled look walks next door to the
Fried Beans Inc. office)

Hey guys, have you heard any more on my special pass?

FBI 1

It has been turned down.

FBI 2

Also, we are no longer going to need your services.

HARVEY

(with a startled look, shrugs, and walks next door
to the Mobs-R-Us office)

So when do we leave for Cuba?

MOBS-R-US AGENT

(tears up business card)

Don't ever contact us again!

HARVEY

(with a startled look, shrugs and walks next door to
the Come C Cuba office)

Have you heard any more on my special travel application?

COME C CUBA CLERK

(rips up Harvey's card)

You are no longer a friend of Cuba!

HARVEY

(looks shocked as he walks into the
CIA Transport office)

Hey guys, I really tried, but I guess my connections aren't what they used
to be. Not sure why, but everyone has turned me down. How are things
going with my special pass application?

CIA 1

We have some bad news for you Harvey.

HARVEY

Let me guess. My special pass has been turned down?

CIA 2

That is true. But there is more.

CIA 1

Harvey, we no longer need your services.

HARVEY

(totally shocked)

What? I have worked for you for a very long time. I have worked hard and done all kinds of special jobs that no one else wanted to do. I have spent lots and lots of time on the road away from my family. This job is how I support my family. Surely there has been some mistake?

CIA 2

No mistake Harvey. Times change, people change, it is time for you to move on.

HARVEY

(The lights dim as the stage is cleared. The spotlight
shines on a despondent Harvey as he walks in circles
at the front of the stage)

What, what happened? I used to be on top...I was the go to guy. I was going up...Everyone wanted me...And now, and now they cast me aside.

(The music starts to "I'm No Longer A Teen"
based on "I'm Eighteen" by Alice Cooper)

More lines on my face and hands

(looks at his hands)

More lines on the Left and Right

(holds out left and right hands)

Still in the middle, without any plans
No longer a boy, they say I'm a man

As a teen
I didn't know what to want
I still don't
Know what I want

(shrugs shoulders)

How do I
Just get away?
I gotta get out of this place
But there's no running in outer space
There's not....

I got an
Older brain, and a colder heart
Took many years to get this far
Don't always know what I'm talking about

(shrugs shoulders)

I'm still living in the middle of doubt
I'm not
A teen
But still get confused every day
Not a teen
Still don't know what to say
How do I
Just get away?

More lines on my face and my hands

(looks at hands)

More lines on the Left and Right

(holds out left and right hands)

I'm in the middle
The middle of life
No longer a boy, but am I a man?
Not a teen
I don't know

(shrugs shoulders)

Oh I don't know
Cause I don't know

(shrugs shoulders)

Should know
Don't know
Should know

Don't know
Help me
Not a teen
But still I don't know

(F, G, and A enter the stage from the left side. They prance around, stop, and circle Harvey. They inspect him closely, look at each other, nod their heads, and start to skip off. Harvey looks bewildered for a moment and then calls out to them.)

HARVEY

(glumly)

Hey, hey wait a minute guys.

(F, G, A stop)

I'd like to talk to you.

(F,G,A tiptoe closer)

I remember seeing you guys in New Orleans. What brings you to Mexico City?

F

Well, we do cover the world.

G

We have been for a long, long time.

A

And we will continue for a long, long time to come.

F

Some say we make good things happen.

G

Some say we make bad things happen.

A

Some say we are the reason for society.

HARVEY

Hold, hold on there. You are getting a little too deep for me. Let's start with the basics, what do F, G, and A stand for?

F

"F" stands for fear. Fear is a very strong motivator.

G

"G" stands for greed. Greed is a very strong motivator.

A

"A" stands for ambition, another very strong motivator.

F

The three of us are kind of like chemicals being mixed together.

G

Sometimes nothing happens.

A

Sometimes something new and useful is formed.

F

And sometimes, everything blows up!

F, G, A

(F, G, and A raise their arms in the air, laugh,
run around in circles, and shout)

BOOM!

HARVEY

I am still a bit puzzled.

F

OK, let's explain it this way.

> (The music starts to "FGA Lite" based on the American
> folk song "Shortening Bread." The audience is asked to
> join the cast in the chorus.)

F, G, A

Fear creates a crisis
Greed and Ambition step in
Things get better
And we start again

Fear creates a crisis
Greed and Ambition step in
Things get better
And we start again

Hurricane's a coming

> (cast member runs across stage flapping a bed sheet)

What we gonna do?
Greed and Ambition
Will take care of you

Wild animals out there

(cast members with animal masks prance around stage)

Give you quite a fright
Greed and Ambition will help you
Sleep through the night

CAST

(motion for audience to join in the singing of the chorus)

Fear creates a crisis
Greed and Ambition step in
Things get better
And we start again

Fear creates a crisis
Greed and Ambition step in
Things get better
And we start again

CIA 1 and CIA 2

Communists are coming
What we gonna do?

CAST

Greed and Ambition
Will take care of you

KGB 1 and KGB 2

Spy planes above you
Give you quite a fright

CAST

Greed and Ambition will help you
Sleep through the night

(motion for audience to join in the singing of the chorus)

Fear creates a crisis
Greed and Ambition step in
Things get better
And we start again

Fear creates a crisis
Greed and Ambition step in
Things get better
And we start again

CUBA 1 and CUBA 2

Illegal aliens are coming
What we gonna do?

CAST

Greed and Ambition
Will take care of you

MAFIA 1 and MAFIA 2

Investments are falling
Give you quite a fright

CAST

Greed and Ambition will help you
Sleep through the night

(motion for audience to join them singing
the chorus, shout out)

Everybody now!

Fear creates a crisis
Greed and Ambition step in
Things get better
And we start again

Fear creates a crisis
Greed and Ambition step in
Things get better
And we start again

DETECTIVE

Taxes are rising
What we gonna do?

CAST

Greed and Ambition
Will take care of you

FBI 1 and FBI 2

Drug gangs are out there
There's going to be a fight

CAST

Greed and Ambition will help you
Sleep through the night

(motion for audience to join in the singing of the chorus)

Fear creates a crisis
Greed and Ambition step in
Things get better
And we start again

Fear creates a crisis
Greed and Ambition step in
Things get better
And we start again

JACK

Health problems coming
What we gonna do?

CAST

Greed and Ambition
Will take care of you

KGB COLONEL

My country's going broke
It's not a pretty sight

CAST

Greed and Ambition will help you
Sleep through the night

(motion for audience to join in the singing of the chorus)

Fear creates a crisis
Greed and Ambition step in
Things get better
And we start again

Fear creates a crisis
Greed and Ambition step in
Things get better
And we start again

GI 1, GI 2, GI 3, GI 4

(shout out first line, sing second line)

Not enough dames out there
What we gonna do?

CAST

Greed and Ambition
Will take care of you

GAL 1, GAL 2, GAL 3, GAL 4

If looking in the mirror

(look in mirrors and have shocked looks)

Gives you quite a fright

CAST

Greed and Ambition will help you
Sleep through the night

(motion for audience to join in the singing of the chorus)

Fear creates a crisis
Greed and Ambition step in
Things get better
And we start again

Fear creates a crisis
Greed and Ambition step in
Things get better
And we start again

KGB GAL

My boyfriend has left me
We had a terrible fight

GI 1, GI 2, GI 3, GI 4

(shout out lines)

Who cares about Greed and Ambition?
I'll help you sleep through the night.

CAST

Fear creates a crisis
Greed and Ambition step in
Things get better
And we start again

Fear creates a crisis

(The music stops and members from the crowd call
out fears. "F" stands at the front center of the stage
and motions for the cast to call out fears)

CROWD 1

Terrorists!

CROWD 2

The economy!

CROWD 3

The health care system!

CROWD 4

AIDS!

CROWD 5

Traffic!

CROWD 6

Mosquitos!

CROWD 7

The Aggies can't win a championship!

CAST

Greed and Ambition step in

("G" and "A" stand in the front center of the stage and
motion for the cast to call out)

CROWD 8

Vote for me!

CROWD 9

Follow me!

CROWD 10

Give to my cause!

CROWD 11

Buy my product!

CROWD 12

It's a good deal!

CROWD 13

Root for UT!

(Music back on. Cast members hold up smiley face signs)

CAST

(special ending music, progressively louder, draw out
second syllable of again)

And...We...Start...AGAIN!

(The cast exits to both sides of the stage. Harvey, F, G,
and A are in the front center of the stage)

HARVEY

Wow! I think I understand. Humans have all kind of fears. In order to overcome the fears, we live in societies. Greed and Ambition motivate our leaders so that we have the military and police to protect us, a medical system to keep us healthy, and factories to produce products for our comforts. It's a wonderful system. You guys are great!

F

Things are good as long as the three of us stay balanced.

HARVEY

What, what do you mean?

G

Greed and Ambition need Fear to survive.

A

And if there is not enough Fear, Greed and Ambition will create a little Fear.

F

Its OK to create a little Fear, some people call it being cautious.

G

But when Greed and Ambition deliberately create a lot of Fear to further their cause…

A

Things can get real ugly. Come, we'll show you.

(lights dim)

Scene Four

The curtains open to a gloomy, gothic stage - a vision of Hell. Ghoulishly dressed performers with "leashes" creep and crawl around the edges of the stage. The music starts to "FGA Heavy" based on "Fire" by Ozzy Osbourne. The song is sung by the Troubadour dressed in a devil costume. Three families consisting of a father, mother, and two children are hiding in "caves" on the front left, front center, and front right of the stage. A rope "leash" is tied around the waist of one of the parents. F, G, and A each grab a leash and pull the parent from the cave. The families are holding hands, and all follow in the direction that F, G, and A pull the parent. The families are taken to three stakes in the middle of the stage. Each family is tied to a stake by F, G, and A. Bundles of hay are placed by the stake. The ghoulish performers hold up screens to block the audience's view of the stakes. During the song, the Troubadour goes behind the screen with a "torch" to light the bonfires and "fire" in the form of flashing red lights is seen from behind the screens.

TROUBADOUR

(loud and frightening)

I AM THE GOD OF HELL FIRE AND I BRING YOU

Fear, it will make you squirm
Greed, it will make you turn

Ambition will burn!
You worked hard and you saved and learned
But all of it's gonna burn
And your mind, your tiny mind
You know you've really been so blind
Now's your time burn your mind
You're falling far too far behind
Oh no, oh no, oh no, oh no, you're gonna burn!

CAST

Fire, to destroy all you've done
Fire, to end all you've become
We'll see you burn!

TROUBADOUR

You've been living like a little girl
In the middle of your little world
And your mind, your tiny mind
You know you've really been so blind
Now's your time to burn your mind
You're falling far too far behind

TROUBADOUR AND CAST

Oh no, oh no, oh no, oh no, oh no, oh no, oh no, oh no

Fear, it will make you squirm
Greed, it will make you turn

You're going to burn!
You're going to burn!
You're going to burn! You're going to burn! Burn! Burn! Burn! Burn! Burn!Burn!
Burn! Burn! Burn!
Fear, it will make you squirm
Greed, it will make you turn
Ambition, makes you yearn
We'll watch you burn

TROUBADOUR

(loud and frightening)

I AM THE GOD OF HELL FIRE, HA, HA, HA, HA, HA, HA, HA, HA, HA, HA, HA, HA, HA

> (Lights dim and the stage is cleared. Harvey, looking upset, paces back and forth in the spotlight taking in everything he has seen. He is joined by F, G, and A.)

F

Well Harvey, what do you think?

HARVEY

(shook up, pauses frequently)

You guys, you guys appear so carefree...But you are bad!...You are beyond bad. You are awful! You destroy families. Those poor kids. They never had a chance. They didn't do anything wrong! Why?

G

That's just our other side.

A

Our intentions are good, but sometimes things don't turn out that way.

HARVEY

Man, I hope I never have to live through a time like that.

F

Don't worry, you won't.

(G and A give him a dirty look)

G

Harvey, you have a new assignment.

A

You are going to Dallas and will have a new job at the Texas School Book Depository.

(lights dim)

Scene Five

The stage is split. On the far left third of the stage is the living room of Harvey and Mariana's home in Dallas, Texas. There is a table, two chairs, a TV, and a rocking horse. On the right side of the stage is the "House Where Evil Deeds Are Done" in New Orleans. It has five offices, each with a desk, two chairs, and a phone. The signs in the offices from left to right are "CIA Transport", "Cuban Cigars", "Mobs-R-Us", "FBI", and "KGB Vodka". The right side of the stage is initially dark. Harvey is watching TV.

MARINA

(walks over to Harvey and gives him hug,
draws out "two")

Harvey, can you believe it? We now have two Texas kids!

HARVEY

(keeps watching TV)

Yes dear.

MARINA

Our youngest child Rachel is one month old! And June is now two years old!

HARVEY

(doesn't look up from watching TV)

Yes dear.

TV ANNOUNCER

This just in. The president will be traveling to Texas next week. On Friday he will be in a motorcade driving through downtown Dallas. A large turn-out is expected. Check your local newspaper for the motorcade route.

MARINA

(excitedly)

Harvey, this is great! You work in downtown Dallas. The president may drive right by your building. You could see the President of the United States of America!

(The lights dim on the left side of the stage and brighten on the right side. The phones ring on each desk. One by one they are answered.)

CIA 1

Dallas? Yes sir, we will have the Ultimate Executive Transport there on Friday.

KGB 1

Dallas? Yes comrade, we will have the Big Shot Executive Vodka there on Friday.

CUBA 1

Dallas? Si Señor we will have the Castro Special Executive Cigars there on Friday.

MAFIA 1

Dallas? Yes sir, we will have the Blow Out Executive Merchandise there on Friday.

FBI 1

Dallas? Got it sir. We will have the Executive Action Paperwork there on Friday.

(The music starts to "When Black Friday Comes" based on the song "Black Friday" by Steely Dan. CIA 1, CIA2, KGB 1, KGB 2, CUBA 1, CUBA 2, MAFIA 1, MAFIA 2, FBI 1, and FBI 2 step out of their offices to the center of the stage to sing and dance. At the end of the song they go back to their offices, grab an arsenal of weapons, and exit.)

CIA 1, CIA 2, KGB 1, KGB 2, CUBA 1, CUBA 2,
MAFIA 1, MAFIA 2, FBI 1, FBI 2

When Black Friday comes
What are you going to do?
There's really no place to hide when it comes for you

When Black Friday comes
Will you purchase a great big gun?

(an enormous gun is brought on stage)

Put your treasures in a bag and hit the road and run
When Black Friday comes you know it's got to be
Don't let it fall on me

When Black Friday comes
Will you take a limousine ride?
Look back on everything you did and say you're satisfied

(FBI 1 and FBI 2 kick off their shoes and
dangle their bare feet)

Say I did just what I please
Sometimes wore no socks and shoes
Didn't do too much but fed lots of kangaroos

(performers hop like kangaroos)

When Black Friday comes I'll be crossing that hill
You know I will

(everyone pretends to dig a hole, Mafia 1 and
Mafia 2 lay down like they are in a grave)

When Black Friday comes
I'm going to dig myself a hole
Then I'll lay down in it 'till I satisfy my soul

The world's going to pass by me
Hope the Archbishop will sanctify me

(everyone looks down on Mafia 1 and Mafia 2 and
walks past them while crossing themselves)

And if he don't come across that's how its gonna be

When Black Friday comes
I'm gonna stake my claim
That things will not be the same

(at the end of the song everyone picks up multiple
weapons from their desks and carries them off stage,
lights dim)

Scene Six

A few days later - Black Friday. Harvey and Mariana's home from the previous scene is on the far left third of the stage. There is a TV, two chairs, a table, and a rocking horse. The right side of the stage is empty and the lights are dim. Mariana is dusting.

MARINA

(to herself)

That Harvey is so lucky. Here I am doing housework, and today he gets to see the President of the United States of America!

(she dusts some more)

I love both my children, but I really love it when they are asleep like they are right now. I think I am going to watch TV for a few minutes and take a nap.

(Mariana sits down in front of the TV
and falls asleep)

TV ANNOUNCER 1

This just in. The president has landed at Dallas Love Field. He is boarding his motorcade for a trip to downtown Dallas.

TV ANNOUNCER 2

This trip is something that he really needs to raise his popularity in the South.

TV ANNOUNCER 1

That's right Bob. Many people in the South don't like the idea, as they say, of having a Catholic Yankee in the White House.

TV ANNOUNCER 2

Yes Chuck. They were pleased when the President selected a Texan for his Vice President in the previous election, but now there are rumors that the Vice President from Texas may not be on the ticket for next year's election.

TV ANNOUNCER 1

Well, politics aside, from the looks of the crowds that have lined the streets to see his motorcade, it looks like Dallas is going to give the president a real southern welcome.

(The lights on the left side of the stage dim. Blue lights shine on both sides of the stage for a dreamlike appearance. A crowd of people enter the right side of the stage. Some are carrying pitchforks and scythes. Others carry guns. Marina stands up and slowly walks towards them.)

MARINA

Where, where am I? Who, who are you? Wait, I know you.

(points at people)

I know who you are. You are the people Harvey works with. What, what
are you doing here?

CROWD 1

(ghost like)

Hurry. The president will be here soon.

MARINA

(excitedly)

You are going to see the president?

CROWD 2

(ghost like)

Hurry up. Get in position. The motorcade is coming.

MARINA

(now noticing the guns)

Why, why do you have guns when you are going to see the president?
Oh no! Oh no! You are not going to...you are not going to shoot the
president...are you?

CROWD 3

(ghost like)

It has to be done.

MARINA

But, but why?

CROWD 4

(ghost like)

It's for the good of the world.

CROWD 5

(ghost like)

It's for the love of my country.

CROWD 6

(ghost like)

It's for the good of the South.

                              CROWD 7

                           (ghost like)

It's for the love of God.

                              CROWD 8

                           (ghost like)

It's for the good of my business.

                              CROWD 9

                           (ghost like)

It's for the Kids.

                              CROWD 10

                          (regular voice)

Hey, I'm getting paid lots of money.

                              MARINA

But he is alive. He is another living human being. You would kill him?

(The music starts to "Are You Going to Assassinate" based on "Are You Going to Celebrate" by Rare Earth. Marina is standing near four "Lone Rangers" dressed identically in blue jeans, white tee shirts, cowboy hats, and "lone ranger" masks. They each carry a rifle and have a rope "leash" tied around their waists.)

LONE RANGERS

One, two, three, four.

MARINA

Are you going to assassinate?
Another human being
Are you going to kill today
In the name of Love?

LONE RANGERS

I'm getting paid by some people
Who want this guy to go down
So the world will go their way it's gonna save the kids, anyhow

That's why I'm telling you
I'm going to assassinate, yeah, yeah
Another human being - yeah!
Yes I am going to kill today in the name of love

MARINA

For the kids are you really going to kill?

For the kids will you kill today?
I can't understand why you don't just...turn away

LONE RANGERS

That's why I'm telling you
I am going to assassinate, yeah, yeah
Another human being, yeah
I'm going to assassinate, another human being
I am going to kill today, in the name of love!

MARINA

What you are doing is wrong, you have got to know
You have got to turn - around and around and around and around and around

Well you can't be bothered with sorrow
And you can't be bothered with hate, oh no
Spend some more time to make others feel fine, every day

LONE RANGERS

Not what I'm telling you
I'm going to assassinate

Oh yeah

I just want to assassinate today
Oh, I am going to assassinate another human being
I am going to kill today in the name of love!

MARINA

Killing is wrong you should really know
You have got to turn around and around and around and
around and around and around, round, round
round, round, round, round, round, round, round, round, round,
round
Don't take him down

(Marina tugs at each of the masks of the Lone Rangers
and asks if they are Harvey)

Harvey, is that you?
Harvey, is that you?
Harvey, is that you?
Harvey, is that you?

(Each Lone Ranger walks away from Marina and
turns their back to the audience while they raise their
guns. Four gunshots are heard. The Lone Rangers
turn back to face the audience.)

LONE RANGERS

Did I just assassinate?
Did I just assassinate?
Well, did I just assassinate?
Say did I just assassinate? Kill today
Did I just assassinate? Did I kill today?
Did I just assassinate? Did I kill today?
Did I just assassinate, Kill today
Did I just assassinate?

(Mariana walks back to her chair and falls asleep. The crowd disappears leaving the right side of the stage empty except for three large signs. "Love and Happiness" points to the left, "Fame and Fortune" points to the right, and "Success" points to the left and to the right. Harvey runs in from the left side of the stage by himself. He stops, reads the signs, and then runs off the right side of the stage. A few seconds later, a group of policemen with billy clubs run in from the left side of the stage, pause on the right side of the stage, and then run off the right side of the stage. Harvey returns from the right side of the stage, starts to run off the left side of the stage, pauses, and runs back to the right. The policemen do the same. Harvey runs to the right side of the stage a third time and is then surrounded by policemen that appear on all sides of him. He is knocked down under the "Success" sign and the policemen pile on top and then escort him in handcuffs off the right side of the stage. The blue lights fade and the stage lights brighten. Marina is talking in her sleep.)

MARINA

(draws out "No's", first syllable of "Harvey", and "me")

No, No, No. Harvey, come back to me. Leave those evil people. No don't take him away from me!

TV ANNOUNCER 1

This just in. We have some sad breaking news. The president has been shot. The president of the United States has been shot today in downtown Dallas.

MARIANA

(now awake and standing up with her hands on her face,
loudly with a very long drawn out "No")

Oh NO!

(lights dim)

Scene Seven

The next day in the Detective's office in the Dallas Police Department. There is a desk with two chairs in the front center of the stage and a large sign that says "Dallas Police Department." The door to the office is on the left side. Police 1 and Police 2 escort Harvey into the office. The Detective is wearing a white suit with blue shirt and red tie.

POLICE 1

Here he is again sir.

POLICE 2

Do you need anything else?

DETECTIVE

Thank you gentlemen. Please wait outside. Hello again Harvey.

HARVEY

Hello, uh, detective?

DETECTIVE

Detective is fine. I am not really a detective. I am more of a crisis fixer. But the guys around here think I am a detective, so I'll go by that.

HARVEY

(F, G, and A appear in the back left corner of the stage.
They dance while Harvey sings and they then exit the
stage on the left side)

Fear creates a crisis, greed and ambition step in, things get better and we start again.

DETECTIVE

What's that?

HARVEY

(draws out "fixed")

Oh, just something I heard. Well, have you fixed the problem?

DETECTIVE

It is getting fixed as we speak.

HARVEY

Great, so you contacted the people I mentioned. How soon can I go home to my wife and kids?

DETECTIVE

Well Harvey, there is good news and bad news.

HARVEY

OK, what is it?

DETECTIVE

The good news Harvey is that you are going to be world famous. People all over the world are going to know your name. And not just now. You are going to be so famous that 50 years from now or even 100 years from now people will know your name.

HARVEY

Well that's great, but why and when can I go home?

DETECTIVE

The bad news Harvey is - you are not going home.

HARVEY

(shocked)

But, but why not? I told you I didn't kill the president and I gave you a
list of people to contact in intelligence agencies that can vouch for me.

DETECTIVE

First off Harvey, this is a police station. Everyone that comes in here
says they are innocent. Secondly, no one is ever going to vouch for you.

HARVEY

What? Why not? I, I don't understand.

CIA 1 and CIA 2

(spotlight shines on CIA 1 and CIA 2 singing in the
back left corner of the stage)

We've given you a number and taken away your name

(CIA 1 and CIA 2 exit on the left side)

DETECTIVE

Harvey, the president of the United States has been killed and you are
the prime suspect. No one is going to admit ever having worked with
you.

HARVEY

(pleading)

But, but you have got to believe me.

DETECTIVE

Harvey, the way I see it, there are three possibilities:

(counting on his fingers)

1. You did it. In which case you are going to be found guilty of murder.

2. You may have helped the people that did it. In which case you are going to
    be found guilty of conspiracy to commit murder which is just as serious,
    because we are talking about the president of the United States, or

3. You have been framed by the people that did it. In which case you
    are going to be found guilty of murder because only a very powerful
    group could have arranged all of this.

HARVEY

So I lose either way.

DETECTIVE

That is correct. You lose. But there is a way to make it not a total loss.

HARVEY

How, how is that?

DETECTIVE

Confess. Sign this written confession.

HARVEY

And how does that make things better?

DETECTIVE

Harvey, no one wants to drag the country through the ordeal of a trial. The country needs to move on.

HARVEY

And how would that help me?

DETECTIVE

Harvey, ask not what your country can do for you, ask what you can do for your country. By signing these papers, you will be doing an extremely great service to your country.

HARVEY

But I'll be dead - executed for killing the president of the United States. Something I didn't do!

DETECTIVE

Maybe or maybe not. There are a lot of powerful people that might prefer that you stay in prison.

HARVEY

(agitated)

Prison for the rest of my life?

DETECTIVE

(calmly)

Harvey, let's try this again. Lots of people will die if a war breaks out. A war that could be prevented by you signing these papers. Harvey, you may be able to stop World War III. Think of the kids. Do you want thousands of kids to go off to war and die? Sign the papers. Do it for the kids. You do want to save the kids, don't you?

HARVEY

Yes, but I didn't...

DETECTIVE

(increasingly loud)

Harvey, the kids need your help. Sign the papers for the Kids! Help SAVE THE KIDS!

MARINA

(While Harvey ponders Marina appears singing in
the spotlight in the back right corner of the stage)

It's for the kids, everyone tells me so
It's for the kids, no, no, no, no

(Marina exits the stage on the right side)

HARVEY

No, no, no, no

I can't sign the papers.

DETECTIVE

Very well.

    (opens the door and addresses the policemen)

Take him back to his cell.

    (they leave and the detective picks up the phone)

It's me again sir. No, he won't play ball.

(The detective hangs up the phone. He stands up and a rope leash around his waist drops to the floor. He goes out the door and exits to the left. Harvey is in the spotlight in the front center of the stage while the stage is cleared. Police 1 and Police 2 are nearby as

Harvey sings "My Intentions Are Good" based on "Don't Let Me Be Misunderstood" written by Benjamin/ Marcus/Caldwell and performed by The Animals.)

HARVEY

Hey there, can you understand me now?
Sometimes I feel a little sad
Well don't you know that no one alive
Can always be an angel
When things go wrong I seem to be the bad

I'm just a soul who's intentions are good
Oh Lord, please don't let me be misunderstood

Hey there, sometimes I appear carefree
My true self I try to hide
And sometimes it seems that
All my life is filled with worry
And then you're bound to see my other side

I'm just a soul who's intentions are good
Oh Lord, please don't let me be misunderstood

If I seem evil, I want you to know
That I never meant it to turn out that way
Life has its problems and I get my share
And there are things I never meant to do

Cause I love life
Oh, oh, oh, hey there, don't you know I'm human
Have thoughts like any other one
Sometimes I find myself alone and regretting
Some foolish thing, some little simple thing I've done

POLICE 1 and POLICE 2

(music stops, Police 1 and Police 2 point fingers at
Harvey and shout)

LIKE SHOOTING THE PRESIDENT!

(music resumes)

HARVEY

I'm just a soul who's intentions are good
Oh Lord, please don't let be misunderstood

Yes, I'm just a soul who's intentions are good
Oh Lord, please don't let me be misunderstood

Yes, I'm just a soul who's intentions are good
Oh Lord, please don't let me be misunderstood

Yes, I'm just a soul who's intentions are good

(lights dim)

Scene Eight

The stage is split with Jack's shabby apartment on the left side and Harvey's jail cell on the right. The apartment has a table, straight back chair, and a sign that says "Welcome to Jack's Place". There is a phone and a handgun on the table. Jack is talking on the phone and petting his black cat "Sheba". The jail cell on the right side of the stage has a cot and a sign that says "Dallas City Jail". The right side of the stage is initially dark.

JACK

I know, I know you would prefer that I had a job that wasn't a nightclub operator...I know, I know some of the people I work with are a bit shady and rough around the edges, but inside they are not all bad. They have many good traits...Well for one, they all like kids. Like the fine ones you are raising...I know, I know, I've got to go too, but I want you to know that you and your kids mean the world to me.

(hangs up the phone and addresses his cat Sheba)

You, Sheba, mean the world to me too.

(phone rings, Jack answers)

Jack's place.

(abruptly stands up)

Hello sir...Yes, I saw it on TV...Well sir, we sure are glad that he is now gone. He and his brother were making things rough on us. Sounds like that Harvey guy did us a real favor...Sure, you know that I would do anything for you.

(with a shocked look)

You want me to do what? But, but why?...Yes, sorry about that sir...Yes, I know that I should never, never ask you why...But they will catch me... They will know that I did it...Yes, I know that a lot of our associates have spent time in jail, but this is Texas. We are talking death penalty! Yes sir, I know that there are worse things than death...

(pleading loudly)

No! No! No! Don't ever mention harming them in any way...OK, I'll do it, but please promise me that you will protect them and take care of them while I am away...When?...Now? They are getting ready to transfer him right now?...OK, OK. I'll be there in a few minutes.

(Jack picks up his gun and stuffs it into his pocket. He turns and picks up his cat and gives it a big hug)

Sheba, my good friend, I am getting ready to do something that will get me arrested and put away for a long, long time. It is for a good cause. It is going to save the kids, some very special kids, but I am going to never ever see you again. Here, let me put you outside one last time.

(He carries Sheba off stage and returns. The music starts and Jack sings "Where Did I Go Wrong?" based on "How Can I Be Sure?" by the Rascals. The music order is first verse, second verse twice, first verse, second verse twice, first verse, second verse twice, first verse.)

Where did I go wrong?
In a world that's constantly changing
Where did I go wrong?
What became of me?

There was a time
When my world was filled...with friends
And the days
They seemed to have no ends

There was a time
Round me the girls...were there
And young love
It always filled the air

Where did I go wrong?
In a world that's constantly changing
Where did I go wrong?
What became of me?

There was a time
When I knew all there was...to know
And the world
It seemed to move so slow

There was a time
I had strength beyond...compare
I could move
The stars from here to there

Where did I go wrong
In a world...that's constantly changing
Where did I go wrong?
What happened to me?

There was a time
I could travel...anywhere
And bright hopes
Around me filled the air

There was a time
I wanted all to know...my name
So that I
Could obtain everlasting fame

Where did I go wrong?
In a world...that's constantly changing
Where did I go wrong?
What became of me?

> (The lights fade on Jack's side of the stage and brighten on Harvey in his jail cell. Harvey has been sitting on his cot. He stands up.)

HARVEY

What happened to me? How did I get into this mess?

(The music starts and Harvey sings "Where Did I Go Wrong?" based on "How Can I Be Sure?" by the Rascals. Harvey walks to the center of the right side of the stage in the spotlight while the lights dim in the jail cell behind him and the set is cleared. The music order is first verse, second verse twice, first verse, second verse twice, first verse, second verse twice, first verse.)

Where did I go wrong?
In a world that's constantly changing
Where did I go wrong?

What became of me?
There was a time
When my world was filled...with friends
And the days
They seemed to have no ends

There was a time
Round me the girls...were there
And young love
It always filled the air

Where did I go wrong?
In a world that's constantly changing
Where did I go wrong?
What became of me?

There was a time
When I knew all there was...to know
And the world
It seemed to move so slow

There was a time
I had strength beyond...compare
I could move
The stars from here to there

Where did I go wrong
In a world that's constantly changing
Where did I go wrong?
What happened to me?

There was a time
I could travel...anywhere
And bright hopes
Around me filled the air

There was a time
I wanted all to know...my name
So that I
Could obtain everlasting fame

Where did I go wrong?
In a world that is constantly changing
Where did I go wrong?
What became of me?

(As the song ends, Police 1 and Police 2 approach Harvey,
and handcuff him)

POLICE 1

Harvey, its time to go.

POLICE 2

You are being transferred to the County Jail.

(They escort him off the right side of the stage. The lights brighten.
A crowd of reporters is on the left side of the stage. Jack slowly walks in
from the left side of the stage. Harvey, escorted by Police 1 and Police
2 slowly enters from the right side of the stage and moves towards the
reporters. Jack and Harvey continue singing "Where Did I Go Wrong?"
based on "How Can I Be Sure?" by the Rascals. The music order is first
verse, second verse twice, first verse, second verse twice, first verse, second verse twice, first verse.)

JACK and HARVEY

Where did I go wrong?
In a world that's constantly changing
Where did I go wrong?
What became of me?

There was a time
When my world was filled...with friends
And the days
They seemed to have no ends

There was a time
Round me the girls...were there
And young love
It always filled the air

Where did I go wrong?
In a world that's constantly changing
Where did I go wrong?
What became of me?

There was a time
When I knew all there was...to know
And the world
It seemed to move so slow

There was a time
I had strength beyond...compare
I could move
The stars from here to there

Where did I go wrong
In a world that's constantly changing
Where did I go wrong?
What happened to me?

There was a time
I could travel...anywhere
And bright hopes
Around me filled the air

There was a time
I wanted all to know...my name
So that I
Could obtain everlasting fame

Where did I go wrong?
In a world that's constantly changing
Where did I go wrong?
What became of me?

(Jack approaches Harvey)

POLICE 1

Hi Jack!

POLICE 2

Hey Jack!

(Jack pulls out his gun and fires a shot in Harvey's left side)

REPORTER

(loud and excited)

He's got a gun!

(Jack fires two more shots into Harvey's left side.
Harvey falls to his knees. Jack is pulled down to his
knees by Police 1 and Police 2. Jack and Harvey finish the song singing to each other from their knees.)

JACK and HARVEY

(music from first verse of "Where Did I Go Wrong?"
based on "How Can I Be Sure?" by the Rascals)

Look at where I am
Cast aside and no longer needed
Anyone out there care?
Will you re... mem... ber me?

(Jack and Harvey collapse to the floor, lights dim)

Scene Nine

The next day in The House Where Evil Deeds Are Done in New Orleans. There are five empty offices that each contain one desk. The office signs have been taken down. There are lots of bags of trash on the sides of the stage. CIA 1, CIA 2, KGB 1, KGB 2, CUBA 1, CUBA 2, MAFIA 1, MAFIA 2, FBI 1, and FBI 2 are seated in chairs in a semicircle in the center of the stage. They are all relaxing, drinking vodka, and smoking cigars.

CIA 1

(pointing to bags)

Shredding all done?

CUBA 1

Si Señor. It took a while, but it is all finished.

KGB 1

Did you all hear what happened yesterday to the guy that shot the USA president?

MAFIA 1

Tragic, totally tragic.

FBI 1

Didn't that guy, what's his name, Harvey, look familiar?

KGB 2

I can't recall.

CIA 2

Maybe you are getting him confused with someone else.

CUBA 2

All gringos look alike.

FBI 2

At least we don't look like your leader – that Castro guy. Who dresses him? He needs a haircut and a shave and why would anyone wear camouflage in downtown Havana?

CUBA 1

So says the FBI agent whose boss wears a dress.

FBI 1

(draws out "Hey")

Hey, don't knock our director. He has files on all of us.

MAFIA 1

(smoking a big cigar)

You know, there are certain things I really miss about Cuba. These cigars aren't legal in the US anymore. Of course that means we can now sell them here for a much higher price.

CIA 1

If you Mafia guys hadn't screwed up, we'd still be in Cuba.

MAFIA 2

Don't look at us. Who botched the Bay of Pigs Invasion? It was you guys, the CIA.

CIA 2

Give him a break. The president announced the attack on TV before it had even started. Who tells the enemy...

(looks over at Cuba 1 and Cuba 2)

uh, no offense guys, in advance that an attack is coming?

KGB 1

Only in America.

CIA 1

Hey, but we kicked Soviet butt in the Cuba missile crisis.

KGB 2

I think you need to work on your definition of who kicked whose butt.
You guys signed an agreement not to attack Cuba and all it cost us was
the freight for a few missiles.

MAFIA 2

Well, that president is now gone. May he rest in peace.

(takes off his hat)

Did we ever figure out who killed him?

(everyone looks puzzled)

FBI 1

Why it was Harvey, of course. Don't you watch the news?

MAFIA 1

Are people really going to believe that Harvey fired four shots in five seconds from a rifle?

FBI 2

Well actually it was only three shots, one of which was a magic bullet.

KGB 1

(shaking his head in disbelief)

A magic bullet? Only in America.

CUBA 1

But won't there be an investigation that shows that it had to be more than one person? Who will get blamed then?

(everyone points fingers at each other and laughs)

CIA 1

Let's face it guys, misinformation is our business. Give them 50 years or 100 or even 1,000 years. There is no way anyone is ever going to unravel this one!

MAFIA 1

Well I guess it is time to move on. Where are you guys heading?

CUBA 2

We're going to Central and South America. You know, do a little bit of the revolution thing. Increase the market for Havana cigars as we like to call it. How about you guys?

(pointing to the FBI)

FBI 1

We go wherever our leashes take us, and all of us here have leashes.

FBI 2

We may chase you Mafia guys for a while, especially if the president's brother becomes president some day. Where are you crooks going?

MAFIA 1

(draws out "Hey")

Hey, I'll have you know that we are respectable businessmen. At least that's the direction our public relations department says we are heading. They are talking about doing a movie about us, something called, "The Godfather". There is supposed to be a killer scene with a horse. I can't wait.

MAFIA 2

Meanwhile, our marketing department tells us there is a lot of money to be made in the narcotics business, so you may see us here and there around the world.

(points to CIA1 and CIA2)

How about you guys?

CIA 1

We are going to an out-of-the way spot far, far away. It used to be known as French Indochina, now it is called Vietnam.

CIA 2

How about our Soviet friends with the good vodka?

KGB 1

Now you know good and well that wherever you go, we go. We are kind of a team. Together we make the world a better place...save the kids and all that.

KGB 2

Our informants tell us that you guys are heading out next week.

CIA 1

Yeah, but was it real information or misinformation?

(They all laugh. F, G, and A skip into the room.
They pause and are greeted by everyone)

CUBA 2

Hey amigos, what's next for you?

F

You know we are all over the world.

G

Always have been.

A

And always will be.

FBI 2

Isn't that the truth.

CIA 2

Well, we are going to Vietnam. Will you guys be there?

NARRATOR

(a deep, loud, booming voice shakes the auditorium)

OH YEAH!

(lights dim)

Scene Ten

The next day at the Dallas city morgue. Two policemen are escorting Marina. Harvey is lying on a stretcher in the middle of the stage. There is a sign that says "Dallas Morgue."

POLICE 1

Here we are ma'am. This is the morgue.

POLICE 2

Would you like some time alone?

MARINA

Yes please.

(The police leave. Marina fidgets and paces and circles Harvey's body. She stops and starts and then looks closely at his face. She turns away in disgust and then comes back to the body. She relaxes a bit and then the music starts and she sings "Harvey" based on "Angie" by the Rolling Stones.)

Harvey, Harvey, why did you have to disappear?
Harvey, Harvey, where will my life go from here?
With your love not in my life, and infamy now as your wife
I can't say I'm satisfied

(shakes head)

But Harvey, Harvey, you can't say we never tried.

Harvey, you're beautiful, but ain't it time we said goodbye?
Harvey, I still love you, remember all those nights we cried?
All the dreams we held so close have now gone up in smoke
Let me whisper in your ear
Harvey, Harvey, where will it lead me from here?

Oh Harvey, don't you weep, all your kisses still taste sweet
I hate that sadness in your eyes
But Harvey, Harvey, ain't it time we said good-bye?

With your love not in my life, and infamy now as your wife
I can't say I'm satisfied

(shakes head)

But Harvey, I still love you Baby, ev'rywhere I look I see your eyes
Your Russian girl wants to be close to you, come on open up your eyes

(puts her hands on his eyelids)

But Harvey, Harvey, if only you were still alive
Harvey, Harvey, they can't say we never tried

(walks to the door, turns, and waves good bye, lights dim)

Scene Eleven

The same day in the Detective's office at the Dallas Police station. There is a desk with two chairs in the front center of the stage and a sign that says "Dallas Police Department." Police 1 and Police 2 escort Marina into the office.

DETECTIVE

(to Police 1 and Police 2)

Thank you. That will be all gentlemen.

(pulls up a chair for Marina)

Thank you for coming Marina. I know this is a very difficult time.

MARINA

You said you had some papers for me to sign. What is this all about?

DETECTIVE

Yes this, what shall we call it, uh event, has received worldwide attention. The press is hounding everyone and asking lots and lots of questions. We need to bring it to a close quickly.

MARINA

Of course they have questions, the same questions I have. Who is behind Harvey's shooting and who really shot the president?

DETECTIVE

People, uh, people that ask these questions are really making life difficult for themselves and others.

MARINA

What, what do you mean?

DETECTIVE

When there is not closure, people are filled with anxiety and become fearful. Think about it, if the President of the United States isn't safe and if the police can't protect someone in their custody, then who really is safe?

MARINA

Well, they are right. There are some very evil people out there that need to be caught and punished.

DETECTIVE

Ideally yes, but what people really want is justice, or at least the appearance of justice. They will get that when we tell them what happened.

MARINA

But you don't know what happened, so what are you going to tell them?

DETECTIVE

Our, uh, evidence suggests that your husband was maybe deranged or maybe he wanted to be famous. Anyway, he found out about the president's motorcade route, brought a gun to work, and shot him from a window in the building where he worked. While he was in police custody, a nightclub operator shot Harvey because he felt sorry for the president's wife and all the grief she would experience if this case went to trial.

MARINA

So a middle aged man, that makes a living serving booze and running a strip club, killed my husband because he wanted to make a lady...

(increasingly loud and incredulous)

that he never met, that lives clear across the country, feel better? That is absurd!

DETECTIVE

I'll admit, it is a little rough around the edges, but if you say it loud enough and long enough, people will believe it and go on with their lives.

MARINA

I can't say much about the nightclub operator, other than he definitely killed my husband. But I do know Harvey. He never liked being the center of attention, he was always a quiet person that adapted to new situations - definitely not the kind of person that seeks attention. And as far as being mad at the president, why shoot someone in America, when you can vote him out of office in next year's elections?

DETECTIVE

I'll admit, that this too has a few rough edges. That's why we need your help.

MARINA

(increasingly loud and incredulous, draws out "you")

My help? Do I look like Sherlock Holmes? I thought it was you people that are going to find the killers.

DETECTIVE

(calmly)

Let me try again, Mariana. There are two separate issues here. One is finding the killer or killers and the other is making the American people, and people around the world, feel safe again by wrapping things up.

MARINA

Wrapping things up? You haven't found the people responsible? Why aren't you searching for them. I know for a fact that my husband traveled to some unusual places and had some business associates that I always thought were a bit shady. You need to question these people and find out what they know. Harvey is being set up to be the fall guy, and they, they probably have something to do with it!

DETECTIVE

I assure you that we are working on it. But, if there were others that pulled the trigger, do you really think that they are still alive?

MARINA

What, what do you mean?

DETECTIVE

If this assassination is part of some kind of conspiracy and the people behind it have enough power to kill the president of the United States as well as someone in police custody, do you think they are going to leave the real killers alone and allow them some day to tell the world the truth?

MARINA

But, but you've got to find out who is responsible. If not, they will kill again.

DETECTIVE

Marina, if Harvey didn't do it, and that is a big if because, as you say, he certainly had some unusual dealings, let's look at the possibilities of who is behind this:

(counting on his fingers)

1. It could be the Soviets…you are from Russia…do you want to start World War III over this?

2. It could be the Cubans…we go to war with them and their ally, the Soviet Union, joins them and again we have World War III.

3. It could be the Mafia…we come down hard on them and then we have open street warfare and lots of people die.

4. It could be some clandestine group in the government, possibly as part of a power struggle…groups in the government start fighting among themselves, the country falls apart, we have a civil war, and lot's of people die.

I assure you – I have put a lot of thought into this. Harvey taking the fall is the best solution.

MARINA

So what do you want from me?

DETECTIVE

I need for you to sign these papers that support our official story and agree not to talk to the press.

MARINA

But Harvey is innocent. Surely people will realize that. If the police can't help I can go to the press to get support.

DETECTIVE

(draws out "Whoa")

Whoa there Marina. You need to realize that there are a lot of powerful people that want this wrapped up quickly and neatly. How long do you think you would be safe? Believe you me, I am thinking only about your best interests.

MARINA

(defiant)

My best interests? I can take care of myself.

DETECTIVE

(pulls out two pictures and hands them to Marina)

Marina, you are 22 years old. You have two young children, one of whom is only one month old, and you have no means of support. We can help you.

MARINA

(Marina takes the pictures and stares at them.
A shocked look appears on her face)

This, this is June and Ra...Rachel. How, how did you get these pictures
of my...my kids?

DETECTIVE

Marina, people everywhere are watching you. By signing these papers,
you will be protecting not only yourself, but also your kids, not to mention kids from all over the world that will suffer if this is not wrapped up
quickly. Marina, think of the kids.

(increasingly loud and forceful)

Do it for the kids! Don't you want to save the kids? Marina, help save the
kids! It's for the kids. Marina, SAVE THE KIDS!

MARINA

(stands up, increasingly loud)

For the kids? For the KIDS? Everybody has a cause and they say it is for
the kids, but who is supporting the cause of my DEAD HUSBAND!

(The music starts and Marina sings "It's Not For the Kids"
based on "Can't Buy Me Love" written by Paul McCartney
and performed by the Beatles)

It's for the kids, no

(shakes head)

Kids no

(shakes head)

It's for the kids, no

(shakes head)

You say you want to go to war, so your kids will be safe at night
Arm your soldiers, make battle plans, give them quite a fight
But your kids don't care a-bout the war, they want you home at night

You say that you are working late, so your kids will have things new
You go on trips make lots of money, that is what you do
But your kids don't care a-bout the money, they want to spend time with you

(next two "kids" are drawn out)

It's for the kids, everybody tells me so

(fires "gun finger" four times during "no's")

It's for the kids, no, no, no, no!

You say that you are helping make - the world a better place
And I think that it is really grand, to save the human race
But your kids don't care a-bout the world, they want to see your face.

(loud and drawn out scream)

STOP!

(music stops and Mariana paces furiously, draws out "no")

I am no different...I have a cause, a really good one...I believe my husband is innocent. But, you are right...I can't fight powerful people, and if I do, many innocent people will die...But my kids, my kids don't care about any of this. All they care about is being loved...I can't change the world, but I can love and take care of my kids!

(Marina signs the papers. There are multiple pages to sign. As she and the Detective are sitting at the desk signing the papers, the music starts to "Save the Kids!" based on "Louie, Louie" by the Kingsmen. A group of parents dressed in business attire for current times enter. They are carrying cell phones, brief cases, and babies (dolls). They walk past Marina and the Detective and scratch their heads wondering what they would have done under the circumstances and are relieved that it is not happening to them. Groups of cast members dressed as kids gather on the sides and front of the stage. The parents walk toward the kids and give them hugs.

Directional signs are placed on the stage. "Love and Happiness" points to the left, "Fame and Fortune" points to the right, and "Success" points to the left and to the right.

After Marina has signed the papers, the Detective stands and escorts Marina out of his office. He puts the signed papers in his briefcase and leaves. He stops to read the directional signs and then follows the "Fame and Fortune" sign for a right exit.

After she has signed the papers, a parent gives Marina her two kids. She hugs June and takes Rachael in her arms, then reads the directional signs and follows the "Love and Happiness" sign, exiting on the left. She stops near the exit, turns and waves good bye to the audience, and exits the stage.

At the end of the song, the modern day parents walk hand-in-hand with their kids and follow the "Success" sign, exiting on the left side of the stage.)

CAST

Oh me, Oh my, Oh no
Which way to go?

(scratching heads)

Aye-yi-yi-yi
Oh me, oh my, oh baby
You're gonna grow

Fine little kids, look to me
To guide them through life's stormy sea
How can I help them, they're all alone
I need to be with them at home

(the parents make a "balancing" motion with their hands
showing how they are trying to balance work and family)

Oh me, oh my, oh no, no, no, no
Which way to go? Oh no

(scratch heads as they look at Marina)

Oh me, oh my, oh baby
You're gonna grow

For nights and days I travel the land
Think of them, they are grand
Why be here, I'm needed there
Got to show them that I care
Oh me, oh my, oh no
Which way to go?

(scratch heads as they look at Marina)

Aye-yi-yi-yi
Oh me, oh my...oh baby
You're gonna grow

Okay, let's spend some time with 'em, right now!

(during the guitar solo the parents play with the kids -
pushing a bicycle, throwing a ball, playing with dolls,
the Detective exits right, Marina exits left with her
kids)

Save 'em

Help save the kids, from fears they got
Help save the kids, they mean a lot
Take them in your arms again
Be with them as much as you can

(parents and kids walk hand-in-hand to the directional
signs and pause to read them)

Oh me, oh my, oh no,
Which way to go?

(scratch heads)

Aye-yi-yi-yi
Oh me, oh me, oh baby
You're gonna grow

(parents and kids walk to the "Love and Happiness"
exit on the left side of the stage)

You're gonna grow up

Let's take it on out of here now
Let's go!

(the curtain closes ending Act 2)

Curtain Call

The curtain opens and the cast members take bows while singing and hamming it up to "Secret Agent" based on "Secret Agent Man" written by Steve Barri and P.F. Sloan and performed by Johnny Rivers. The audience is asked to join in the singing.

CAST and AUDIENCE

There's a man who leads a life of danger
To everyone he meets he stays a stranger
With every move he makes another chance he takes
Odds are he won't live to see tomorrow

Secret Agent Man
Secret Agent Man
They've given you a number and taken away your name

Beware of pretty faces that you find
A pretty face can hide an evil mind
Oh be careful what you say
Or you will give yourself away
Odds are you won't live to see tomorrow
Secret Agent Man
Secret Agent Man
They've given you a number and taken away your name

Secret Agent Man
Secret Agent Man
They've given you a number and taken away your name

Swinging nightlife in Clute Texas one day
Spying undercover in Russia after that
Oh be careful what you say
Or you will give yourself away
Odds are you won't live to see tomorrow

Secret Agent Man
Secret Agent Man

They've given you a number and taken away your name
Secret Agent Man

CAST

(shout)

SAVE THE KIDS!

(The curtain closes. As the applause subsides, a loud, deep booming voice once again shakes the auditorium)

NARRATOR

OH YEAH!

About the Author

Andrew J. McNabb is a native Texan and was in Dallas when JFK was shot. He remembers being in his second grade classroom when the principal announced to the school that the president had died.

After graduating from Texas Tech University with a degree in Chemical Engineering, Andrew moved to Lake Jackson, Texas. During his career in the chemical industry, he picked up 12 patents and lots of interesting stories.

Andrew and his wife Sharon have two beautiful daughters Jennifer and Kristin and a menagerie of pets. The family enjoys seeing the world and have had many travel adventures. When not engineering, writing, or traveling, Andrew enjoys sports and is an avid chess player.